*The Kierkegaard-Girard Option*

MERCER UNIVERSITY

MERCER UNIVERSITY PRESS

*Endowed by*

TOM WATSON BROWN

*and*

THE WATSON-BROWN FOUNDATION, INC.

# *The Kierkegaard–Girard Option*

CHARLES K. BELLINGER

MERCER UNIVERSITY PRESS
*Macon, Georgia*
1979–2019
40 Years of Publishing Excellence

MUP/ P592


Published by Mercer University Press
1501 Mercer University Drive
Macon, Georgia 31207


9 8 7 6 5 4 3 2 1

Books published by Mercer University Press are printed on acid-free paper that meets the requirements of the American National Standard for Information Sciences—Permanence of Paper for Printed Library Materials.

Printed and bound in the United States.

This book is set in Adobe Caslon Pro.

ISBN 978-0-88146-724-6
Cataloging-in-Publication Data is available from the Library of Congress

# Contents

# Acknowledgments

Particular thanks go out to Woody Belangia and George Dunn for their assistance in drafting Chapter 3, "Kierkegaard and Mimetic Theory." Professors Ann George and Richard Enos of Texas Christian University were of great assistance to me in studying the thought of Kenneth Burke and rhetorical theory more generally. The members of the professional societies that I have participated in have offered helpful feedback and general camaraderie on many occasions. I refer here to the Kierkegaard Society within the American Academy of Religion, the Colloquium on Violence and Religion, University Faculty for Life, and the Society of Catholic Social Scientists.

*The Kierkegaard-Girard Option*

# Introduction

Rod Dreher's *The Benedict Option*[1] has provoked much commentary and response. It has struck a chord, particularly with social conservatives, who feel that they have "lost the culture wars" with regard to such issues as abortion, same-sex marriage, and freedom of conscience protections. Dreher advises his fellow conservatives to engage in a strategic retreat into enclaves of the like-minded, to weather out a storm of persecution from cultural liberals that may last for decades. The specter of the Soviet experiment, which lasted from 1917 to 1989, haunts his prose.

Dreher advises his readers to look to monasticism as a model to be emulated in the new dark ages of liberal hegemony. He does not mean this with strict literalism, but in a broad sense; Christian families and churches should adopt routines of daily prayer and Bible reading that are modeled after the practices of medieval monasteries. He suggests that believers should, whenever possible, choose to live in close vicinity with other members of their congregation, and share their lives together in mutual support and accountability. Parents should pull their children out of public schools, which have become a toxic wasteland of bad influences from teachers and students who are morally corrupted, and either home school their children or form or attend pre-existing Christian schools. Traditionalists should be prepared for the reality that certain lines of work that were open to them in the past will no longer be possible because of the moral compromises and pressures to conform to new liberal orthodoxies that would be required of them in those lines of work. Christians must live lives of high moral probity and resist the technologizing of almost all aspects of modern culture. Traditional believers must become counter-cultural, echoing the monks and nuns of the Middle Ages, and in other ways the Amish and the Bruderhof.

This rough and inadequate summary of Dreher's message does not do it justice, of course, but it does serve to provide an orientation for the reader of this book who has not read that book. While I am in sympathy with much of what Dreher says and would likely strike up a warm friendship with him if our lives crossed paths, my purpose in this book is to express an alternative framework for looking at our contemporary situation. My arguments,

[1] Rod Dreher, *The Benedict Option: A Strategy for Christians in a Post-Christian World* (New York: Sentinel, 2017).

developed in the chapters that follow, are not attacking his, as much as they are seeking to add new ideas and perspectives that he does not address.

Violence, for example, takes many different forms in our world: wars and rumors of wars, ethnic cleansing, mass shootings, terrorist attacks, and on and on. The call to Christians to be peacemakers in a violent world is a continual call from God, and it requires outreach, mission, and witness, not retreat into enclaves. It is my firm belief, which only grows deeper with time, that the Christian message is uniquely positioned to shed a powerful light of understanding and reconciliation in precisely this aspect of human culture. This will be my main message in the pages below, drawing on Søren Kierkegaard (1813–1855) and René Girard (1923–2015), with supplementary insights from Kenneth Burke (1897–1993).

The abortion debate receives some attention from Dreher, but I think he underestimates its importance. If—engaging in a purely hypothetical thought experiment—the legalization of abortion in the modern West is a philosophical house of cards, then that house will come crashing down some day. Christians ought not to wait passively for that time; they ought to be card pullers. This should not be motivated by a desire to "win" this aspect of the culture wars, but by a deep yearning to save souls from enslavement to what is in fact yet another form of violence. The pro-life movement needs to take encouragement and guidance from the Abolitionist movement of the nineteenth century, knowing that grave philosophical errors can last for centuries, but they can also be repudiated and transcended. Othering—interpreting a group or class of human beings as being outside the moral community—is to a great extent the original sin of humanity, and Christians ought to always be on the offensive against it, confident that God provides the true antidote to original sin.

Another aspect of our current cultural situation that needs attention is illuminated well in Girard's writings, namely that liberalism is parasitic upon the tradition that it claims to have transcended. Any movement for social change in the modern world has to claim that it is on the side of victims and is adept at recognizing and denouncing victimizers. But the thought that cannot be conceived by today's liberals is that their sensitivity to victimization is itself the fruit of biblical revelation. There is an amnesia at work here, a forgetting of the roots of ideas. To use rights language as a rhetorical club to attack one's opponents, for example, without giving one nanosecond of thought to the roots of the concept of rights in the West, is to climb out on a limb that cannot support one's weight. The Christian tradition is not just a limb; it is in fact the strong trunk of the tree that has produced rights language. This is another area where Christians should adopt the stance of being on offense, not defense.

In general, modern culture, with its polyphony of worldviews, is a grand contest centered around the key question: What are the moral lessons that we ought to learn from history and how will we live when we have learned those lessons rightly? Christians are dwellers in history, or at least they ought to be. It is the moderns, the liberals, who try to escape from history into the dream of radical individualism and nominalist self-creation. Here, also, it ought to be easy for Christians to hold the high ground when it comes to learning the lessons of history.

One key lesson that we ought to have learned from Gandhi and Martin Luther King, Jr. is that *truth is a force in history*. It may seem like a weak force much of the time, but appearances can be deceptive. This is a point perceived clearly by Kierkegaard, who said that the eternal—God—is like a great cliff that scatters the sea foam. It matters not to God whether the number of human beings who are fleeing from truth and toward falsehoods is ten, ten million, or ten billion. Truth is never determined by crowds; it determines itself and speaks forth itself.

That "the crowd is untruth" is a truth enunciated by Kierkegaard, and that phrase serves as a perfect summary of Girard's thought as well. Why should these two thinkers be seen as an "option" for us today? I seek to persuade my reader in the pages that follow that these two authors are extraordinarily insightful teachers from whom we need to learn. We need to learn about the deepest roots of violence from them, because it is only in that specific area of learning that humanity will be able to take its next great step forward. Copernicus is a symbol of the great step forward of learning about the non-living aspects of the cosmos. Darwin is a symbol of the great step forward of learning about the living creatures.[2] What remains the deepest mystery, however, is the task of understanding ourselves as human beings. Anthropology is the last great frontier. From Kierkegaard and Girard we can learn not just important truths about anthropology through thinking about violence; at a deeper level we can come to understand that the pathway to genuine understanding must first travel deep into history before coming back into the present, changed. And when we complete that journey we will understand ourselves with a fullness of wisdom as physical, social, historical, moral, sexual, and spiritual beings—made in the image of God—and called and loved forth into being by the living God.

[2] I am pointing to Charles Darwin as a symbol, not implicitly supporting "Darwinism" or entering into the debate about "intelligent design," etc.

An autobiographical section of this introduction is necessary to round out the picture. I was born and raised in the evangelical Protestant world; as a middle-aged adult I was received into the Catholic Church. I am, like Dreher, a "traditionalist," as that term is bandied about today. But I have spent most of my adult life in academic circles that are "liberal," as that term is bandied about. I have one foot in both camps, and I have always sought to open up lines of communication between the camps, though that is a thankless task. I have sought to make conservatives more understandable to liberals and vice versa. I have sought to comfort the afflicted and afflict the comfortable on both sides. For the past nineteen years I have been a faculty member at a liberal Protestant seminary, after having gone through graduate education in similarly liberal settings. The "fit," as the saying goes in academia, is less than ideal. But God has put me in this situation and I try to do my best in it. Kierkegaard and Girard are so important to me precisely because they strike me as thinkers who transcend our small-minded divisions. They are authors who are respected and drawn upon by both conservatives and liberals. What is needed, I have concluded, is not retreat into enclaves but better quality conversations about the way forward for the United States and for the world. And the only way we will have better quality conversations is if the voices we listen to are those whose insights transcend the shoutings of the demagogues of both the right and the left.

* * *

A word about the arrangement of the chapters below. The book begins with my translation from the Danish of an important short essay by Kierkegaard on the theme: "the crowd is untruth." This is followed by an essay by Girard, "The First Stone," reprinted with permission from the journal *Renascence.* In the essay Girard contrasts two events of stoning by crowds, one encouraged by Apollonius of Tyana, the other prevented by Jesus. The similarity between the arguments of Kierkegaard and Girard will be apparent to the reader.

I gave a talk at the Girard society (the Colloquium on Violence and Religion) in 1995. I argued that there is a deep consonance between Kierkegaard and Girard in their interpretation of human psychology. Girard was present in the audience and he came up to me afterward and expressed agreement with what I had argued. Chapter three of the present book is basically rewriting from scratch that talk, after more than twenty years of further reading and reflection.[3] My central arguments are that Kierkegaard would have fit in perfectly as a sixth author considered within Girard's *Deceit, Desire, and the Novel*,[4] and that "Kierkegaard has Girard surrounded"—meaning that Kierkegaard sees mimetic desire and scapegoating, but he also analyzes the roots of human sin much more deeply than Girard does, and he has much more to say about the process of spiritual growth than Girard does.

This is followed by a talk I gave not long after the 9/11 attacks, in which I claim that Kierkegaard should be seen as the spiritual Copernicus of our age; I suggest Karl Barth and Girard as the analogues of Kepler and Galileo, though in other essays below I employ Kenneth Burke or Eric Voegelin rather than Barth as an analogue to Kepler. Whether we are drawing on a theologian or philosopher is less important than the substance of their penetrating critiques of the malaise of modernity. Just as the astronomers radically de-centered human beings as observers of the cosmos, so also do we need today a de-centering of human beings as justifiers of their own violence.

I include two substantive essays on Kenneth Burke because he is an intrinsically thought-provoking and substantive commentator on the human condition, and his thought is not well known among the readers of Kierkegaard or Girard. Many readers of Girard, for example, will be surprised to learn that Burke, not Girard, coined the phrase "the scapegoat mechanism" (in the 1930s). Burke also serves well the goal of improving the quality of conversation in our context today, because those readers who count themselves among the "nones" ought to read Burke and take him seriously. Burke was not a "religious" person himself; he was a secular intellectual, but he did not adopt the annoying atheistic fundamentalism of Richard Dawkins and his ilk. He was respectful toward religious people and ideas, and he was wrestling very deeply with the idea that human culture is at the same time unavoidably "religious" and also enmeshed in cathartic acts of violence. He is an important voice to consider in the project of improving human self-understanding.

The essay on Girard and the Batman movie *The Dark Knight* demonstrates how the ideas of Girard are not "ivory-tower" speculations, but profoundly illuminative of a widely viewed product of popular culture. This es-

---

[3] The original talk was published as "'The Crowd is Untruth': A Comparison of Kierkegaard and Girard." *Contagion: A Journal of Violence*, Mimesis, and Culture 3 (1996): 103–19.

[4] The other five are Cervantes, Stendhal, Flaubert, Proust, and Dostoevsky.

say can also serve to lead the reader to think more carefully about the issue of the unjustified use of force by the police, which is a very prominent aspect of contemporary American culture.

The next chapter, "Kierkegaard's Critique of Individualism," focuses on what I have come to call "dimensional anthropology," which is the idea that there are three main dimensions that human beings inhabit: the vertical axis (God and nature), the horizontal plane (social relations), and individual selfhood. These dimensions were seen clearly by Kierkegaard, and his overall message draws the reader into inhabiting the dimensions in a rich way, which is the opposite of modern individualism.

The concluding chapter seeks to explicate the title of the book. I use three books as foils, in the sense that they are popular books that suggest what the reading public considers to be sound scholarship and helpful contributions to contemporary debates: *Terror in the Mind of God*, by Mark Juergensmeyer, *The Righteous Mind*, by Jonathan Haidt, and Kate Greasley's contribution to a debate book called *Abortion Rights: For and Against*. I find these texts to be philosophically defective in various ways as they try to address religion and violence, moral psychology, and the abortion debate. I explain what I find problematic in these texts, and I bring in other authors who have provided more insightful and philosophically sound perspectives on these important topics. Juergensmeyer will be responded to by Richard Weaver, René Girard, and Eric Voegelin. Haidt will be responded to by Servais Pinckaers, Shelby Steele, and Daryl Koehn. Greasley will be responded to by Chantal Delsol, Giorgio Agamben, and Søren Kierkegaard.

So what is the Kierkegaard-Girard Option? These bullet points begin to outline the answer:

- We *must* think about the question "Why are human beings violent?" The luxury of ignorance is no longer possible. This question needs to be asked as a society-wide inquiry, built into our curricula at the high school and college levels, and also in seminaries. This is the crucial element in the New Copernican Revolution.
- The abortion debate will take a turn in a strongly pro-life direction at some point in the future, because the pro-choice worldview arises out of the philosophical falsity of othering. We need to prepare as a culture for this major change.
- The debate over same-sex marriage will likely be a "We will have to agree to disagree" situation for a long time into the future. Thinking about the difference between parallel vs. conflictual competition will be helpful. Which worldview leads to healthier communities that contribute to the flourishing of human lives?

The notion that "liberals" can "win" the culture wars and then become oppressors of "conservatives" is not a viable pathway into the future.

Those on the cultural left and right need to find ways to have more productive conversations going into the future; these conversations need to be informed by the insights of the most subtle and brilliant anthropological thinkers of the modern world, such as Kierkegaard and Girard.

* * *

The central paradox of Dreher's *The Benedict Option* is this: If the learning that is pursued in the Christian community leads to a deepened awareness of the Great Commission, to "go out and make disciples of all nations," then the enclave is undone at the same time as it is established. What it means to make disciples, I claim, cannot be in any sense "business as usual." It must be a discipleship that is informed by the writings of the best and the brightest of the modern age, our contemporary evangelists and apostles, such as Kierkegaard and Girard.

# 1

# On the Dedication to "That Single Individual"

*by Søren Kierkegaard*[1]

Translated by Charles K. Bellinger

My dear, accept this dedication; it is given over, as it were, blindfolded, but therefore undisturbed by any consideration, in sincerity. Who you are, I know not; where you are, I know not; what your name is, I know not. Yet you are my hope, my joy, my pride, and my unknown honor.

It comforts me that the right occasion is now there for you, which I have honestly intended during my labor and in my labor. For if it were possible that reading what I write became worldly custom, or even to give oneself out as having read it, in the hope of thereby winning something in the world, that then would not be the right occasion, since, on the contrary, misunderstanding would have triumphed, and it would have also deceived me, if I had not striven to prevent such a thing from happening.

This, in part, is a possible change in me, something I even wish for, basically a mood of soul and mind, which does not produce change by being more than change and therefore produces nothing less than change; it is rather an admission, in part a thoroughly and well thought-out view of "life," of "the truth," and of "the way."

There is a view of life which holds that where the crowd is, the truth is also, that it is a need in truth itself, that it must have the crowd on its side.[2] There is another view of life; which holds that wherever the crowd is, there

---

[1] [Kierkegaard's notes:] This, which is now considerably revised and enlarged, was written and intended to accompany the dedication to "that single individual," which is found in *Upbuilding Discourses in Various Spirits*. Copenhagen, Spring 1847.

[2] Perhaps, however, it is right to note once and for all, that which follows of itself and which I have never denied, that in relation to all temporal, earthly, worldly ends the crowd can have its validity, even its validity as a decisive court of last resort. But I am not speaking about such things, which I pay so little attention to. I speak of the ethical, the ethical-religious, of "the truth," and seen ethico-religiously the crowd is untruth, when it is taken as a valid court of last resort for what "the truth" is.

is untruth, so that, for a moment to carry the matter out to its farthest conclusion, even if every individual possessed the truth in private, yet if they came together into a crowd (so that "the crowd" received any *decisive*, voting, noisy, audible importance), untruth would at once be let in.[3]

For "the crowd" is untruth. Eternally, godly, Christianly, what Paul says is valid: "only one receives the prize," [1 Cor. 9:24] not by way of comparison, for in the comparison "the others" are still present. That is to say, everyone can be that one, with God's help—but only one receives the prize; again, that is to say, everyone should cautiously have dealings with "the others," and essentially only talk with God and with himself—for only one receives the prize; again, that is to say, the human being is in kinship with, or to be a human is to be in kinship with the divinity. The worldly, temporal, busy, socially-friendly person says this: "How unreasonable, that only one should receive the prize, it is far more probable that several combined receive the prize; and if we become many, then it becomes more certain and also easier for each individually." Certainly, it is far *more probable*; and it is also true in relation to all earthly and sensuous prizes; and it becomes the only truth, if it is allowed to rule, for this point of view abolishes both God and the eternal and "the human being's" kinship with the divinity; it abolishes it or changes it into a fable, and sets the modern (as a matter of fact, the old heathen) in its place, so that to be a human being is like being a specimen which belongs to a race gifted with reason, so that the race, the species, is higher than the individual, or so that there are only specimens, not individuals. But the eternal, which vaults high over the temporal, quiet as the night sky, and God in heaven, who from this exalted state of bliss, without becoming the least bit dizzy, looks out over these innumerable millions and knows each single individual; he, the great examiner, he says: only one receives the prize; that is to say, everyone can receive it, and everyone ought to become this by oneself, but only one receives the prize. Where the crowd is, therefore, or where a decisive importance is attached to the fact that there is a crowd, *there* no one is working, living, and striving for the highest end, but only for this or that earthly end; since the eternal, the decisive, can only be worked for where there is one; and to become this by oneself, which all can do, is to will to allow God to help you—"the crowd" is untruth.

[3] Perhaps, however, it is right to note, although it seems to me to be almost superfluous, that it naturally could not occur to me to object to something, for example that there is preaching, or that "the truth" is proclaimed, even though it was to an assembly of a hundred thousand. No, but even if it were an assembly of just ten—and if there should be balloting, that is, if the assembly were the court of last resort, if the crowd were the decisive factor, then there is untruth.

A crowd—not this or that, one now living or long dead, a crowd of the lowly or of nobles, of rich or poor, etc., but in its very concept[4]—is untruth, since a crowd either renders the single individual wholly unrepentant and irresponsible, or weakens his responsibility by making it a fraction of his decision. Observe, there was not a single soldier who dared lay a hand on Caius Marius; this was the truth. But given three or four women with the consciousness or idea of being a crowd, with a certain hope in the possibility that no one could definitely say who it was or who started it: then they had the courage for it; what untruth! The untruth is first that it is "the crowd," which does either what only *the single individual* in the crowd does, or in every case what *each single individual* does. For a crowd is an abstraction, which does not have hands; each single individual, on the other hand, normally has two hands, and when he, as a single individual, lays his two hands on Caius Marius, then it is the two hands of this single individual, not after all his neighbor's, even less—the crowd's, which has no hands. In the next place, the untruth is that the crowd had "the courage" for it, since never at any time was even the most cowardly of all single individuals so cowardly, as the crowd always is. For every single individual who escapes into the crowd, and thus flees in cowardice from being a single individual (who either had the courage to lay his hand on Caius Marius, or the courage to admit that he did not have it), contributes his share of cowardice to "the cowardice," which is: the crowd. Take the highest, think of Christ—and the whole human race, all human beings, which were ever born and ever will be born; the situation is the single individual, as an individual, in solitary surroundings alone with him; as a single individual he walks up to him and spits on him: the human being has never been born and never will be, who would have the courage or the impudence for it; this is the truth. But since they remain in a crowd, they have the courage for it—what frightening untruth.

The crowd is untruth. There is therefore no one who has more contempt for what it is to be a human being than those who make it their profession to lead the crowd. Let someone, some individual human being, certainly, approach such a person, what does he care about him; that is much too small a thing; he proudly sends him away; there must be at least a hun-

[4] The reader will therefore recall, that here by "crowd," "the crowd" is understood as a purely formal conceptual definition, not what one otherwise understands by "the crowd," when it supposedly is also a qualification, when human selfishness irreligiously divides human beings into "the crowd" and the nobles, and so forth. God in heaven, how would the religious arrive at such in-human equality! No, "crowd" is the number, the numerical; a number of noblemen, millionaires, high dignitaries, etc.—as soon as the numerical is at work, the "crowd" is "the crowd."

dred. And if there are thousands, then he bends before the crowd, he bows and scrapes; what untruth! No, when there is an individual human being, then one should express the truth by respecting what it is to be a human being; and if perhaps, as one cruelly says, it was a poor, needy human being, then especially should one invite him into the best room, and if one has several voices, he should use the kindest and friendliest; that is the truth. When on the other hand it was an assembly of thousands or more, and "the truth" became the object of balloting, then especially one should godfearingly—if one prefers not to repeat in silence the Our Father: deliver us from evil—one should godfearingly express, that a crowd, as the court of last resort, ethically and religiously, is the untruth, whereas it is eternally true, that everyone can be the one. This is the truth.

The crowd is untruth. Therefore was Christ crucified, because he, even though he addressed himself to all, would not have to do with the crowd, because he would not in any way let a crowd help him, because he in this respect absolutely pushed away, would not found a party, or allow balloting, but would be what he was, the truth, which relates itself to the single individual. And therefore everyone who in truth will serve the truth, is *eo ipso* in some way or other a martyr; if it were possible that a human being in his mother's womb could make a decision to will to serve "the truth" in truth, so he also is *eo ipso* a martyr, however his martyrdom comes about, even while in his mother's womb. For to win a crowd is not so great a trick; one only needs some talent, a certain dose of untruth and a little acquaintance with the human passions. But no witness for the truth—alas, and every human being, you and I, should be one—dares have dealings with a crowd. The witness for the truth—who naturally will have nothing to do with politics, and to the utmost of his ability is careful not to be confused with a politician—the godfearing work of the witness to the truth is to have dealings with all, if possible, but always individually, to talk with each privately, on the streets and lanes—to split up the crowd, or to talk to it, not to form a crowd, but so that one or another individual might go home from the assembly and become a single individual. "A crowd," on the other hand, when it is treated as the court of last resort in relation to "the truth," its judgment as *the* judgment, is detested by the witness to the truth, more than a virtuous young woman detests the dance hall. And they who address the "crowd" as the court of last resort, he considers to be instruments of untruth. For to repeat: that which in politics and similar domains has its validity, sometimes wholly, sometimes in part, becomes untruth, when it is transferred to the intellectual, spiritual, and religious domains. And at the risk of a possibly exaggerated caution, I add just this: by "truth" I always understand "eternal truth." But politics and the like has nothing to do with "eternal truth." A politics, which in the real sense of "eternal truth" made a serious effort to bring "eternal truth" into real life, would in the same second show itself to be in the highest degree the most "impolitic" thing imaginable.

The crowd is untruth. And I could weep, in every case I can learn to long for the eternal, whenever I think about our age's misery, even compared with the ancient world's greatest misery, in that the daily press and anonymity make our age even more insane with help from "the public," which is really an abstraction, which makes a claim to be the court of last resort in relation to "the truth"; for assemblies which make this claim surely do not take place. That an anonymous person, with help from the press, day in and day out can speak however he pleases (even with respect to the intellectual, the ethical, the religious), things which he perhaps did not in the least have the courage to say personally in a particular situation; every time he opens up his gullet—one cannot call it a mouth—he can *all at once* address himself to thousands upon thousands; he can get ten thousand times ten thousand to repeat after him—and no one has to answer for it; in ancient times the relatively unrepentant crowd was the almighty, but now there is the absolutely unrepentant thing: No One, an anonymous person: the Author, an anonymous person: the Public, sometimes even anonymous subscribers, therefore: No One. No One! God in heaven, such states even call themselves Christian states. One cannot say that, again with the help of the press, "the truth" can overcome the lie and the error. O, you who say this, ask yourself: Do you dare to claim that human beings, in a crowd, are just as quick to reach for truth, which is not always palatable, as for untruth, which is always deliciously prepared, when in addition this must be combined with an admission that one has let oneself be deceived! Or do you dare to claim that "the truth" is just as quick to let itself be understood as is untruth, which requires no previous knowledge, no schooling, no discipline, no abstinence, no self-denial, no honest self-concern, no patient labor! No, "the truth," which detests this untruth, the only goal of which is to desire its increase, is not so quick on its feet. Firstly, it cannot work through the fantastical, which is the untruth; its communicator is only a single individual. And its communication relates itself once again to the single individual; for in this view of life the single individual is precisely the truth. The truth can neither be communicated nor be received without being as it were before the eyes of God, nor without God's help, nor without God being involved as the middle term, since he is the truth. It can therefore only be communicated by and received by "the single individual," which, for that matter, every single human being who lives could be: this is the determination of the truth in contrast to the abstract, the fantastical, impersonal, "the crowd"— "the public," which excludes God as the middle term (for the *personal* God cannot be the middle term in an *impersonal* relation), and also thereby the truth, for God is the truth and its middle term.

And to honor every individual human being, unconditionally every human being, that is the truth and fear of God and love of "the neighbor"; but ethico-religiously viewed, to recognize "the crowd" as the court of last resort in relation to "the truth," that is to deny God and cannot possibly be to love "the neighbor." And "the neighbor" is the absolutely true expression for human equality; if everyone in truth loved the neighbor as himself, then would perfect human equality be unconditionally attained; every one who in truth loves the neighbor, expresses unconditional human equality; every one who is really aware (even if he admits, like I, that his effort is weak and imperfect) that the task is to love the neighbor, he is also aware of what human equality is. But never have I read in the Holy Scriptures this command: You shall love the crowd; even less: You shall, ethico-religiously, recognize in the crowd the court of last resort in relation to "the truth." It is clear that to love the neighbor is self-denial, that to love the crowd or to act as if one loved it, to make it the court of last resort for "the truth," that is the way to truly gain power, the way to all sorts of temporal and worldly advantage—yet it is untruth; for the crowd is untruth.

But he who acknowledges this view, which is seldom presented (for it often happens, that a man believes that the crowd is in untruth, but when it, the crowd, merely accepts his opinion *en masse*, then everything is all right), he admits to himself that he is the weak and powerless one; how would a single individual be able to stand against the many, who have the power! And he could not then want to get the crowd on his side to carry through the view that the crowd, ethico-religiously, as the court of last resort, is untruth; that would be to mock himself. But although this view was from the first an admission of weakness and powerlessness, and since it seems therefore so uninviting, and is therefore heard so seldom: yet it has the good feature, that it is fair, that it offends no one, not a single one, that it does not distinguish between persons, not a single one. A crowd is indeed made up of single individuals; it must therefore be in everyone's power to become what he is, a single individual; no one is prevented from being a single individual, no one, unless he prevents himself by becoming many. To become a crowd, to gather a crowd around oneself, is on the contrary to distinguish life from life; even the most well-meaning one who talks about that, can easily offend a single individual. But it is the crowd which has power, influence, reputation, and domination—this is the distinction of life from life, which tyrannically overlooks the single individual as the weak and powerless one, in a temporal-worldly way overlooks the eternal truth: the single individual.

*Note* The reader will recall, that this (the beginning of which is marked by the atmosphere of its moment, when I voluntarily exposed myself to the brutality of literary vulgarity) was originally written in 1846, although later revised and considerably enlarged. Existence, almighty as it is, has since that time shed light on the proposition that the crowd, seen ethico-religiously as the court of last resort, is untruth. Truly, I am well served by this; I am even helped by it to better understand myself, since I will now be understood in a completely different way than I was at the time, when my weak, lonely voice was heard as a ridiculous exaggeration, whereas it can now scarcely be heard at all on account of existence's loud voice, which says the same thing.

# 2

# THE FIRST STONE

*by René Girard*[1]

The following essay compares two texts that revolve around the same unpleasant but highly significant subject, collective stoning. The first one, located in the Gospel of John, is the famous episode of an adulterous woman whose stoning is prevented by Jesus. The early manuscripts do not contain this text. Many observers find it is more Lucan than Johannine. Whatever the case may be, its content is so unquestionably Christian that its scriptural authenticity is never questioned:

> The scribes and Pharisees led forward a woman who had been caught in adultery, and made her stand there in front of everybody. "Teacher," they said to him, "this woman has been caught in the very act of adultery. Now, in the Law Moses ordered such women to be stoned. But you—what do you say about it?" (They were posing this question to trap him so that they could have something to accuse him of.) But Jesus simply bent down and started drawing on the ground with his finger. When they persisted with their questioning, he straightened up and said to them. "The man among you who has no sin—let him be the first to cast a stone at her." And he bent down again and started to write on the ground. But the audience went away one by one, starting with the elders; and he was left alone with the woman still there before him. So Jesus, straightening up, said to her, "Woman, where are they all? Hasn't anyone condemned you?" "No one, sir." she answered. Jesus said, "Nor do I condemn you. You may go. But from now on, avoid this sin." (John 8.3–11)

The prescription that makes adultery a capital crime applied only to women. At the time of Jesus, it had become controversial and was not always observed. Jesus is in a difficult position therefore. He cannot condone the stoning without betraying his own principles but, if he opposes it, he will be accused of contempt for the Law. The sentence he finally utters when his questioners insist, is one of the most famous in all four Gospels:

*If there is one of you who has not sinned, let him cast the first stone.*

---

[1] Reprinted, with permission, from Renascence 52, no. 1 (Fall 1999): 5–17.

In all languages of old Christendom, such expressions as "the first stone," "to cast the first stone," are very much alive. What can they mean in a world where the practice of stoning has been discontinued? Is the idea of the first stone really significant?

If we pose this question to the language obsessed critics of our time, they will come up with their usual answer. "The first stone," they will say, is a "rhetorical," a "purely rhetorical" device. We all thirst for significance and these critics' greatest pleasure is to disappoint us and make it clear that we, too, must be deconstructed. To them, even though language is everything, it is also nothing at all; it only gives "to airy nothing a local habitation and a name."

We cannot repeat "the first stone" nowadays, without remembering the innumerable repetitions behind us. Let us call this self-consciousness rhetorical, if we like the term but can we thus empty it of all significance? I do not think so. The first stone is still as powerful today, I believe, as when Jesus first used the expression.

How can we show this effectively? However great the Gospel text is, it will not suffice. The reason is simple. Because the sentence we want to explore was too influential, the first stone was never cast. The stoning did not occur.

In order to understand the role of the first stone, we need a second text, preferably independent from the Gospels and from Christianity itself, a text in which the first stone is actually cast and the consequences become visible. Such a text will teach us perhaps, why Jesus emphasized *the first stone.*

The second text I want to discuss is exactly what we need. It is thoroughly pagan. It portrays the actual stoning of an old beggar in the city of Ephesus. This horrible deed is supposed to have been instigated by Apollonius of Tyana, a famous spiritual leader of the second century A.D., a kind of guru we might say. Pagan circles found his "miracles" superior to those of Jesus.

The most spectacular of these, undoubtedly, is the Ephesus stoning. Whereas Jesus cured only one individual at a time, Apollonius is supposed to have cured the entire city with one single trick which turns out to be the stoning of that poor beggar. The account of this collective murder takes up a whole chapter in *The Life of Apollonius of Tyana,* a book authored by Philostratus, a third century Greek writer of some merit:

> When the plague began to rage in Ephesus, and no remedy sufficed to check it, they sent a deputation to Apollonius, asking him to become physician of their infirmity; and he thought that he ought not to postpone his journey, but said: "Let us go." And forthwith he was in Ephe-

> sus,....He....called together the Ephesians, and said: "Take courage, for I will today put a stop to the course of the disease." And with these words be led the population entire to the theatre, where the images of the Averting god had been set up. And there he saw what seemed an old mendicant artfully blinking his eyes as if blind, and he carried a wallet and a crust of bread in it; and he was clad in rags and was very squalid of countenance. Apollonius therefore ranged the Ephesians around him and said: "Pick up as many stones as you can and hurl them at this enemy of the gods." Now the Ephesians wondered what he meant, and were shocked at the idea of murdering a stranger so manifestly miserable; for he was begging and praying them to take mercy upon him. Nevertheless Apollonius insisted and egged on the Ephesians to launch themselves on him and not let him go. And as soon as some of them began to take shots and hit him with their stones, the beggar who had seemed to blink and be blind, gave them all a sudden glance and showed that his eyes were full of fire. Then the Ephesians recognized that he was a demon, and they stoned him so thoroughly that their stones were heaped into a great cairn around him. After a little pause Apollonius bade them remove the stones and acquaint themselves with the wild animal which they had slain. When therefore they had exposed the object which they thought they had thrown their missiles at, they found that he had disappeared and instead of him there was a hound who resembled in form and look a Molossian dog, but was in size the equal of the largest lion: there he lay before their eyes, pounded to a pulp by their stones and vomiting foam as mad dogs do. Accordingly the statue of the Averting god, namely Hercules, has been set up over the spot where the ghost was slain.[2]

A more dismal miracle is hard to imagine! If the author were Christian, scholars would disdainfully dismiss his account as a fabrication, a piece of anti-pagan propaganda. Philostratus was a propagandist all right, but against Christianity. He wanted to show his fellow pagans, demoralized by the progress of the new religion, that there was still life in the old one. His book was quite successful. Which explains why, in the following century, Julian the Apostate revived it. He used it as a weapon in his last ditch battle to save paganism.

Even though the expression "the first stone" appears nowhere in the text we just read, it is relevant, obviously, to the understanding of the whole "miracle." The only moment when the undertaking of Apollonius is in doubt is at the very beginning, before the first stone is cast. Initially, the hopeful Ephesians are quite docile. When Apollonius asks them to form a circle

---

[2] Flavius Philostratus, *The Life of Apollonius of Tyana, The Epistles of Apollonius and the Treatise by Eusebius with an English Translation by F.C. Conybeare*, Loeb Classical Library, Vol. 1 (Cambridge, Mass.: Harvard University Press, 1948) 363–67.

around the beggar, they do. When he asks them to pick up stones, they pick them. But when he orders them to cast their stones at the poor wretch, they simply refuse. However obedient they were before, now they dare rebel against their guru. They even criticize explicitly the idea that the beggar should be stoned.

Although Philostratus is unconditionally committed to Apollonius, he is candid enough to acknowledge this rebellion and even to tell us how the Ephesians justify it. They are "shocked at the idea of murdering a stranger so manifestly miserable." However ugly, useless and disgusting the beggar is, the Ephesians regard him as a fellow human being and they cannot murder him in cold blood. This reasoning makes more sense to the modern reader, of course, than the senseless violence of Apollonius.

This first reaction of the Ephesians is the only ray of light in an otherwise uniformly somber story. The sinister guru quickly extinguishes it. He exhorts his flock vehemently and he finally manages to get the stoning started against the poor beggar whom, with ridiculous grandilo quence, he calls: "this enemy of the gods."

The Ephesians end up stoning the beggar with such zeal that we are not merely saddened but astonished by their sudden metamorphosis. Is it really possible that people who behaved decently an instant before, could become so inhuman in so short a time? How can we account for this amazing transformation?

The answer to this question lies in the expression we are investigating. Before the first stone, everything was in doubt. If the hesitation of the Ephesians had persisted, Apollonius' plan would have failed. As soon as he persuades one of the Ephesians finally to cast the first stone, everything changes.

Even though none of us, I suppose, has ever witnessed a stoning, we all find it easy, curiously, to reconstitute the scene that Philostratus does not describe. After the first stone, a short silence followed, and then a second stone reached the beggar, almost immediately followed by a third, a fourth, a fifth, etc. The stones kept coming faster and faster until the instant when, suddenly, all remaining stones were cast simultaneously. And this was not the end: feverishly now, all the Ephesians picked up more stones and they all tried to outdo each other in stoning efficiency. They did not stop until "their stones were heaped into a great cairn around [their victim]."

Why is the first stone so difficult to cast and why are the following ones so easy? The answer is evident. The first stone is the most difficult because there is no model to imitate. Is a model really necessary for such a simple task as throwing a stone? When the target is a human being it obviously helps. And several models help even more. The more numerous the models, the more the rhythm and intensity of the stoning increases. But the first stone alone is decisive. Once it is cast, the tidal wave begins. All reason and compassion swiftly disappear. Violence and deception triumph. The worries of Apollonius are over.

The whole process is *mimetic*, or *imitative* but, in Philostratus, there are no direct and explicit indications of that fundamental fact. We need Jesus and his idea of the first stone to understand how the initial humanity of the Ephesians could turn so quickly to unspeakable ferocity.

In order to explain the mechanics, or rather the "mimetics" of collective stoning, Jesus does not resort to such abstract words as imitation, mimesis, and the like. He mentions the first stone and that is enough.

If the expression is still alive in our world, even though the practice of stoning has disappeared, the reason is not primarily rhetorical. This expression is not even metaphoric, it is a concrete example of the strange power of violent imitation. In a world where violence is primarily non-physical, "psychological," this power remains very much the same as in the ancient practice of stoning.

Our two scenes begin with two entirely different situations equally unfavorable to the two opposite goals of the protagonists. Apollonius wants to trigger a stoning for which his crowd is obviously not quite ready. Jesus wants to prevent a stoning for which his crowd, or at least part of it, is only too ready. One reason for this readiness, of course, is that the adulterous woman, unlike the beggar, is a real culprit, legally punishable by stoning.

Apollonius desperately wants the first stone to be cast, and Jesus desperately wants it not to be cast. These two opposite goals explain the opposite tactics of the two men. Apollonius refrains from mentioning the first stone by name. If he did, he might increase the resistance to the purely mimetic and mechanical impulse which he wants to trigger. His language is duplicitous. He does not want to focus his listeners' attention on the firstness of the first stone, on the responsibility incurred by the individual who casts it.

Most of our actions are mimetic in a mechanical sense. They consist in doing more or less automatically and unconsciously, what everybody around us is already doing. It is easy, therefore, to join a violent process already started; to start this process oneself is an entirely different proposition.

In my opinion, not only violence but desire itself is essentially imitative or mimetic. If it were not, desire would be more or less instinctual and unchanging. There would be no such things as freedom, language, culture and religion itself.

If mimetic desire is responsible for many specific features of humanity, it is fundamentally good but, when we imitate the desires of those we admire, we are bound to desire the objects they themselves desire. The normal consequence is fierce rivalry for the possession of these objects. The mimetic nature of our desire accounts for our conflictual propensities more effectively than any of the supposedly "scientific" explanations, such as the belief in a purely "biological aggressiveness" that would be greater in the human race than in the other primates.

Philostratus is not an insignificant writer. There are indications in his book that he understands the true nature of the crisis his favorite guru was asked to resolve. Just before the stoning, he inserted a little text that I interpret as an introduction to this "miracle."

This text is a speech by Apollonius. Just before leaving for Ephesus, the great man was sojourning in a harbor. A large ship was about to sail and the guru observed with interest the final preparations for its departure. Each sailor devoted all his care exclusively to the specific task assigned to him. As a result, the whole job was performed most efficiently:

> Now if any single member of this community abandoned any one of his particular tasks or went about his naval duties in an inexperienced manner, they would have a bad voyage and would themselves impersonate the storm: but if they vie with one another and are rivals only with the object of one showing himself as good a man as the other, then their ship will make the best of all havens, and all their voyage will be one of fair weather and fair sailing, and the precaution they exercise about themselves will prove to be as valuable as if Poseidon, our lord of safety, were watching over them.

Human communities are doing well, Apollonius claims, as long as their citizens *vie with each other and are rivals only... in their particular tasks*. Rivalries are good, in other words. provided they do not spread indiscriminately across professional and social boundaries. The people who transgress these boundaries impersonate the storm. Apollonius is warning us against rampant mimetic rivalries. Immediately after this text, I repeat, with almost no transition, the miraculous stoning occurs. This composition suggests, I feel, that Philostratus, without explicitly contradicting the Ephesians, wants to inform us that the epidemic cured by Apollonius was no bacterial plague after all but a social crisis of the type described by Apollonius, a crisis in which all citizens *impersonate the storm*.

The rivalries born of mimetic desire are really what Hobbes calls "the war of all against all." According to the mimetic theory, these crises really "plague" archaic societies and, from the beginning, they would have destroyed all of them or rather prevented them from ever coming into being if some natural counterforce had not been at work to suppress or at least to alleviate them.

Mimetic conflict must spontaneously generate its own antidote. The "miracle" of Apollonius suggests that this antidote could be some form of collective violence against a substitute victim. It is this antidote that Apollonius tries to reactivate against the old beggar and he finally succeeds.

As soon as a victim can be found, upon whom everybody will agree, not for rational reasons but because of a mimetic tidal wave against him/her, the populace feels better. Apollonius is "successful" because, thanks to his stoning, the dynamics of scapegoating which are re-unitive, re-constructive, replace the dynamics of rivalry which are divisive and destructive.

Ever since J. G. Frazer, it has become customary to name all expulsion rituals such as the *pharmakos* ritual, after the best known among them, the scapegoat ritual of Leviticus 16. Because the victim is an animal instead of a man, the scapegoat of the Jews is less shocking than the *pharmakos* of the Greeks, quite legitimately so, but the active principle is the same: the hostilities that ferment inside the community are dissipated against an expendable victim, one whose violent elimination will not inflame the spirit of vengeance within the community. This violence *purges* the community of its "impurities." This is the original meaning of the Aristotelian *catharsis*.

Far from being an illegitimate extrapolation, our modern use of the word scapegoat embodies, I believe, a uniquely modern and Christian understanding of the process which underlies not only the original scapegoat ritual of Leviticus 16, not only all expulsion rituals in archaic societies (as J. G. Frazer came close to discovering in *The Golden Bough*) but also the non-ritualized expulsion phenomena which, to a large degree, continue to structure our world.

The modern meaning of scapegoating demystifies the illusion embodied in the mimetic process, the illusion of a genuinely impure or guilty victim, the illusion that makes the violence effective. Before the first stone was cast, the Ephesians rejected this illusion. They refused to believe that the beggar was the "demon of the plague." As soon as the stoning started, however, they became convinced that Apollonius was right. The violent contagion of scapegoating is an intellectual and spiritual contamination which is easy to observe in the text of Philostratus.

In archaic societies, scapegoating was so intense, I believe, that the victim was spontaneously lynched, (and stoning, of course, is a form of lynching.) Every lyncher felt as if he had destroyed his own personal enemy and, after this paroxystic violence, peace automatically descended upon the whole community.

This is what a careful examination of myths and rituals reveals. After a great deal of violence, the return of peace was such a blessed relief that the beneficiaries felt infinite gratitude to the bringer of that peace who was identified as the victim himself, or herself, the original scapegoat.

From then on, therefore, this original scapegoat was regarded not merely as a malevolent demon, a genuine culprit, but also as an all-powerful benefactor. This is the genesis of archaic religion. The "miracle" of Apollonius is an incomplete but highly suggestive adumbration of the mythico-ritual process.

The benefits of the original scapegoating were so great that all human communities did their best to reproduce the whole phenomenon with substitute victims, for the purpose of protecting themselves from a return of internal strife. They did this in the name of the original scapegoat, regarded as a divinity. This is what we call ritual sacrifice.

The most ancient rituals must have been fairly similar on the whole to the scene portrayed by Philostratus. They must have consisted in the violent destruction of a substitute victim analogous to the unfortunate beggar selected by Apollonius for that same role.

When we look at our miracle closely, we see that it greatly resembles the famous or infamous Greek ritual of the *pharmakos* always performed during the Thargelia festival, perhaps on other occasions as well. Not only was the purpose of the ritual the same as in our case but the victim, (or the two victims) were of the same type as the beggar and they, too, were stoned.

The *pharmakoi* were all derelicts, vagabonds and other socially insignificant people, often afflicted besides, with physical ailments and infirmities, people whose death would not be mourned by anyone and would not further inflame the spirit of revenge. To make sure that suitable victims would be available when needed, many Greek cities kept future victims at public expense. To the ancient Greeks, it seems, the killing of these human victims did not matter much more than the killing of the farm animals used in most sacrifices.

In *La pharmacie de Platon*,[3] however, Jacques Derrida observes that, even though Plato freely uses its cognates, he never uses *pharmakos* itself, the word that designates the human victim. This silence is probably significant.

The beggar selected by Apollonius has all the typical features of a *pharmakos*. Apollonius, obviously, had never laid eyes on him before he entered the theater. His choice was random, therefore, but only up to a point. The guru was too knowledgeable, of course, to select as his victim one of the solid citizens of Ephesus! He knew that his choice had to fall within the range of *pharmakos* acceptability.

How could he guess that he would find a suitable victim in the theater? The public buildings of ancient cities were full of beggars and this is the reason, I suppose, why our astute miracle worker took his crowd to the theater rather than to some lonely place outside the city.

Far from inventing something alien to Greek culture, Apollonius reverted to the specifically Greek modality of scapegoat rituals which had probably been discontinued at long last in the second century A.D., but, contrary to what our scholars enamored with the Greeks confidently assert, this ritual was not so outmoded as yet that, occasionally, it could not be revived.

I interpret the Apollonius miracle as an improvised *pharmakos* ritual which is threatened with failure at first but, when the Ephesians' initial reluctance to stoning is overcome, it becomes so successful that it seems miraculous.

It is interesting to note that Philostratus, whose perspicacity we just observed in regard to the cause of it all, mimetic rivalries, is completely blind to the mimetic trick of collective violence. His insight does not extend to the scapegoat mechanism.

Even though Philostratus shrewdly perceives the mimetic nature of the problem, he does not perceive the mimetic nature of the solution. Just like the Ephesians, he is the dupe of Apollonius. It may well be that Apollonius himself is the dupe of his own miracle!

In order to reach the truth, we must read the miracle of Apollonius as we just did, in the light of Jesus' emphasis on the first stone. If one wants to prevent the stoning, rather than trigger it, it makes sense to focus the attention of the potential lynchers on that last obstacle in the path of contagious lynching. Jesus magnifies the first stone as much as he can by mentioning it explicitly, at the very end of his very brief but very powerful statement. He

[3] Girard is referring to a book by Jacques Derrida published in English translation as *Dissemination* (Chicago: University of Chicago Press, 1983).

wants his words to resonate as long as possible in the ears of his listeners. Instead of hiding the truth, he publishes it.

As long as the obstacle of the first stone remains standing, the mimetic tidal wave is held back. As long as the people hesitate, they can look inwards and reflect on how similar they are to their intended victim. When Jesus suggests that only a man without sin should feel entitled to cast the first stone, he knows full well that, if these people honestly examine themselves, they will discover how similar they are to the adulterous woman. They will be ashamed of killing a fellow human being for an action they themselves commit with total impunity.

The Gospel process is not a miracle but a victory for justice and humanity, which human beings, unfortunately, have been unable to achieve by themselves. They need the Judeo-Christian revelation to give up stoning entirely.

There is a mimetic element, of course, in the dissolving of the crowd, just as in its gathering. Up to a point, the unanimity against stoning recalls the unanimity of stoning but it occurs without sudden acceleration, without the frantic stampede that stoning becomes when everybody joins in.

The would-be lynchers came all together, as a united crowd and "they went away one by one, beginning with the elders." This last detail is fascinating. It shows that, even though the mimetic factor is still present, it is no longer paramount. There is an objective difference as well that makes certain listeners of Jesus more amenable to his teaching than others, the difference of age. The elders are more easily convinced to renounce violence, more aware that they too are sinners, just like the adulterous woman. Experience has diminished their self-righteousness and also perhaps the fierceness of their desires. Instead of the mindless unanimity of the mob, we watch genuine individuals emerging from the crowd. The Gospel text can be read almost allegorically, as the emergence of genuine personhood out of the primordial mob.

The mimetic concept of the first stone is powerfully used by Jesus, but it is not original with him. It comes from the Law which says that, in all indictments which might result in someone being stoned, there should be at least two witnesses against the accused and however convincing their case may be, it is not enough. If the victim is supposed to be stoned, the two accusers are required to cast the first stones themselves. Only afterwards, are the people invited to cast their stones as well.

Legal stoning originates in mimetic scapegoating, no doubt. Like all cultural institutions, it is a by-product of primordial lynching, but it is not simply identical with it.

Even though the Mosaic Law must still rely on the mimetic unanimity of stoning for its official form of capital punishment, unavoidable in the absence of modern judicial institutions, it already emphasizes individual responsibility as much as it possibly can, given the circumstances. The obligation for the two accusers to cast the first two stones is intended to discourage irresponsible accusations.

Since Jesus is against stoning altogether, his teaching transcends the letter of the Law but it is faithful to its spirit in the sense that it is inspired by the Law. This is obviously the case for the sentence we are discussing: "The man among you who has no sin—let him cast the first stone." In order to renounce mimetic contagion entirely, Jesus radicalizes the prescription of the Law which seeks to ward off the most dangerous aspects of mimetic contagion.

The success of Jesus' intervention in favor of the adulterous woman must not lead us to believe that he is primarily a manipulator of crowds, the counterpart of Apollonius in our other text. As a rule Jesus is unsuccessful with crowds and his failures often result in attempts to stone him, which anticipate the crucifixion. His true counterpart in our pagan text is the murdered beggar.

In any society, if one intervenes in favor of unanimously condemned victims, one must expect, in the end, to become a scapegoat oneself, and this is what ultimately happens to Jesus in the crucifixion. He constantly identifies with all the scapegoats of his society and of all societies, especially the most wretched, the most persecuted, like the Ephesus beggar. The truth of that identification can be verified, among other ways, in a small but curious similarity between Jesus' behavior in the Gospel scene we just read, and the beggar's behavior in Philostratus.

When Jesus is questioned about the adulterous woman, instead of confronting the crowd directly, he bends down and starts drawing or writing on the sand. Jesus did not bend down in order to write, I believe, but be writes because he has bent down. Why has he bent down? In order not to look back at those people who look intently at him.

Jesus' goal is to save the woman threatened with death, and he does his best to avoid even the slightest hint of visual provocation. If Jesus returned their looks, these people would probably read in his own eyes, as in a mirror, the anger which is really theirs but which they would project against him. The stoning of the woman would become more difficult to avoid.

Jesus is as prudent as possible and the beggar exemplifies a cruder version of that same prudence. Seeing himself surrounded by men armed with stones, who all look at him searchingly, the beggar "artfully [blinked] his eyes as if blind." Like Jesus, he does not want to seem arrogant. The danger that Jesus senses, in exchanging glances with the crowd, the beggar senses as well. He, too, tries not to provide the people who surround him with pretexts for casting their stones at him.

When the first stones hit him, the beggar opens his eyes, of course; there is no point in keeping them shut any more. He hopes against all hope to find a route of escape. His strategy of avoiding eye contact has failed but its very failure confirms its overall soundness. The crowd automatically interprets the terror in his eyes as proof that the beggar really is the demon identified by Apollonius:

> As soon as some of them began to take shots and hit him with their stones, the beggar who had seemed to blink and be blind, gave them all a sudden glance and showed that his eyes were full of fire. Then the Ephesians recognized that he was a demon....

Philostratus sounds like an intelligent and even a decent man, except when it comes to scapegoating. The stoning does not horrify him. The old pagan faith in guilty scapegoats still possesses him. He has not read the Gospels or, if he has, he has not yet assimilated them.

Neither has Eusebius, it seems. The great historian of the Church, the friend of Constantine, wrote a polemical essay against Apollonius, but the modern reader does not find in it what he expects from a Christian, a resounding indictment of Apollonius' contempt for human life, some awareness that the very idea of Jesus resorting to stoning in order to perform a miracle is ludicrous.

Instead of emphasizing the unbridgeable gulf between Apollonius and Jesus, Eusebius turns the comparison into a mimetic rivalry between miracle workers, just like the pagans. He makes it easier for us to understand why Jesus minimizes his miracles, discourages all references to them.

The principal reason why we ourselves apprehend what neither Philostratus nor Eusebius really apprehend, the horror of scapegoating, is that, whether we are Christians or not, we have assimilated, at least in part, the teaching about the first stone, the teaching of Christ about victims and persecutions, which is present everywhere in the Gospels, of course, and which culminates in the four accounts of the Passion.

In order to show once and for all that human culture is rooted in misunderstood scapegoating, Jesus becomes the willing scapegoat of the crowd and he, too, is mistaken for a culprit by his persecutors.

The Passion and Crucifixion are very much the same mimetic process as the "miracle" of Apollonius, the same collective transference against an innocent victim, but instead of being written in the spirit of the persecutors, also called in the Gospels the spirit of *Satan*, a word which means the successful but deceptive *accuser* of innocent victims, they are inspired by another Spirit entirely, the Holy Spirit, also called the *Paraclete*, a word which means the *lawyer for the defense*, the defender of wrongly accused victims.

Unlike the miracle of Apollonius, the four accounts of the Passion reveal the whole truth of scapegoating, the same truth as in the rest of the Gospels but more complete and explicit than anywhere else. Ever since the Cross, human beings have been struggling with its truth. Even when they acknowledge it, they elude it in part, even when they reject it, part of it nevertheless reaches them. The truth of the Cross will ultimately prevail.

# 3

# Kierkegaard and Mimetic Theory

Søren Kierkegaard[1] and René Girard are both widely read and influential authors in the contemporary academic world, but they are only rarely discussed in relation to each other. The goal of this essay is to persuade the reader that this situation could and should be different, because the two authors share certain core assumptions about the human condition, and the cross-fertilization of ideas in their writings is potentially very fruitful for readers of both thinkers. Both authors, for example, ground their message in the idea that the motivations of human beings are usually hidden from themselves, and that this hiddenness needs to be reflected on in relation to the deepest wellsprings of violence in human culture. To understand oneself more clearly requires a transformed relationship with one's own personhood, and it is only through this dynamic of conversion that the individual will gain some distance from the violence that forms and sustains human culture. In this essay I will briefly introduce Kierkegaard's thought, and show how it is in tune with and in some ways expands upon Girard's concerns.

Though Kierkegaard is a well-known author, a brief introduction to him will be useful to those who know him by name and reputation only, or through reading a small portion of his writings. He lived from 1813–1855, making him a contemporary of Karl Marx, Frederic Chopin, Gustave Flaubert, Fyodor Dostoevsky, and Hans Christian Andersen, who he knew personally. The youngest of seven children born to a wealthy Copenhagen businessman and his wife, he was an extraordinarily brilliant thinker whose works have made a huge impact on modern thought, though that impact was not felt until many decades after his death. This delay was due mainly to the fact that he published in Danish, but also to the inherent difficulty involved in deciphering the meaning of his complicated authorship.

While the life expectancy during that age was certainly less than in ours, his family was unusually hard hit, with five of his six siblings and his

---

[1] "Surren Kyierkagoar" is a rough approximation, for English speakers, of how his name is pronounced by native Danish speakers. The author thanks Woody Belangia and George Dunn for helpful comments on this essay.

father and mother all having passed away by the time Søren was twenty-five. "Remember that thou art dust" was not for him a pious abstraction, but a lived reality.

Kierkegaard's pietistic father wanted him to become a Lutheran minister, and he did complete the educational prerequisites for that occupation, but his main vocation in life was to be an author who wrote fiction, philosophy, and theology. The inheritance left by his father allowed him the luxury of being a full-time author, and he was extraordinarily prolific. During his most active years, 1843-1851, he published roughly twenty-five books. The fiction strand of the authorship did not consist of "novels" in the usual sense of the word, but rather of pseudonymously authored books or parts of books, "written" by imaginary authors. *Either/Or*, *Repetition*, and *Stages on Life's Way* are representative here. Søren's broken-off engagement with Regine Olsen was an anguishing experience for him; it inspired the fictional strand in various ways. The "philosophy" strand was also pseudonymous, as in works such as *The Concept of Anxiety*, *Philosophical Fragments*, *Concluding Unscientific Postscript to the Philosophical Fragments*, and his meditation on Abraham's near sacrifice of Isaac, *Fear and Trembling*. The latter straddles the fiction/philosophy boundary in the sense that it can be read as a reflection on his choice to "sacrifice" his relationship with Regine out of a sense of God's call to him to be an author; yet it is also a highly philosophical reading of Genesis 22. I have been placing stress on the concept of pseudonymity because it is crucial to rightly interpreting these texts. Kierkegaard explicitly said that these imaginary authors do not represent his own personal view of reality; they could not possibly do so because they are disparate and sometimes contradictory voices. They are reminiscent of the cacophony of voices that one would find in a novel by Dostoevsky.

Kierkegaard's own voice is expressed more clearly in his later works, such as *Upbuilding Discourses in Various Spirits*, *Works of Love*, and *Christian Discourses*. These books, and others, communicated in his "sermonic" writing style, through which he became a kind of literary pastor-at-large to the country of Denmark. The discourses typically begin with a passage from the Bible and unpack its meaning at a leisurely pace. Think, for example, of thirty pages on the meaning of the word "you" in "you shall love your neighbor as yourself," followed by thirty pages on "shall" and thirty more on "neighbor"; with all ninety being on "love." Two key late works, *The Sickness unto Death* and *Practice in Christianity*, are pseudonymous, but in such a thin way that reading them as expressing Kierkegaard's own views is surely correct. These works, and others toward the end of his life, articulated his increasingly ardent message that European Christendom was spiritually hollowed out from the inside and on the verge of collapse. His call for a "reintroduction of Christianity into Christendom"[2] went unheeded in Denmark, and in Europe more broadly, as the late nineteenth and twentieth centuries unfolded. In the midst of Kierkegaard's furiously polemic jeremiad, his "attack upon Christendom" in 1855, he collapsed in the street, was carried to hospital, and died within a few days.

Kierkegaard's message can be distilled down into three main ideas: (1) what is wrong with human beings, (2) the process of psychological growth that remedies this wrongness, and (3) the call to love the neighbor as oneself that will be heard by the person who is growing psychologically.

(1) The most important text that explicates the first point is *The Sickness unto Death*. The first half of this dense and striking treatise focuses on "despair" understood psychologically; the second half focuses on "sin" which is the same concept, but understood theologically. Human beings are in despair in that they exist in a state of resistance to the possibility of their own grown in psychological maturity; the text describes this as "not willing to become oneself." Because the human condition consists of existence within polarities (the infinite and the finite, the eternal and the temporal, freedom and necessity), to not become oneself in a true and authentic way means to refuse to hold the poles together in a creative tension. Thus, Kierkegaard describes how an individual may fly off into the "infinite" and avoid the "finite," or vice versa. The many different ways that human beings can avoid growth into maturity accounts for the many different forms of distorted psychology that we see around us in the modern world.

A deep point of contact with Girard's thought is seen here, in that Kierkegaard argues that when human beings are fleeing from the possibility of growth, they huddle together in groups; they form alliances, crowds, mobs. For example:

> Whereas one kind of despair plunges wildly into the infinite and loses itself, another kind of despair seems to permit itself to be tricked out of its self by "the others." Surrounded by hordes of men, absorbed in all sorts of secular matters, more and more shrewd about the ways of the world—such a person forgets himself, forgets his name divinely understood, does not dare to believe in himself, finds it too hazardous to be himself and far easier and safer to be like the others, to become a copy, a number, a mass man.[3]

---

[2] Kierkegaard, *The Point of View* (Princeton: Princeton University Press, 1998) 123.

[3] Kierkegaard, *The Sickness unto Death* (Princeton: Princeton University Press, 1980) 33–34.

This flight into "safety" by joining a crowd is not a mere human foible, an innocuous trait of human psychology; it is actually the engine that drives violence. Kierkegaard recognizes this in *The Sickness unto Death* when he argues that when the ideal of selfhood is presented to human beings in the person of Christ, he is killed. The crowd seeks to "stick together" and to defend itself against the call to growth in selfhood; but "...should there happen to be an individual who dares to speak otherwise...then let us protect ourselves by regarding him as mad or, if necessary, by putting him to death. If many of us do it, then there is no wrong. It is nonsense, an antiquated notion, that the many can do wrong."[4] The psychological need of crowds to attack scapegoats arises out of the resistance of the individuals who make up the crowd to move forward into the process of psychological maturation.

(2) There are various places in Kierkegaard's authorship where he speaks of the process of growth in selfhood, but I will concentrate my necessarily brief remarks here on *Upbuilding Discourses in Various Spirits*, Part One, which is often referred to as "Purity of Heart Is to Will One Thing." This lengthy sermonic treatise calls its reader to cease trying to hide in the crowd, to desist from evading the task of becoming an individual before God. "The eternal," meaning the judgment of the individual spiritually and ethically, is the end of all evasions, all excuses, all ability to stick together with others in a group. Before the Creator "the individual looks around in vain for the crowd."[5] The concept of "purity of heart" means the maturation and unification of the self that is only made possible by becoming a "single individual." In the language of *The Sickness unto Death*, which was written later, this is "becoming oneself before God." Many readers of Kierkegaard encounter this theme in his writings and immediately jump to the accusation that he is guilty of atomistic "individualism." This is a mistaken critique when we consider *Works of Love*, which we will turn to next, but even in this text, "Purity of Heart," Kierkegaard anticipates and heads off this criticism:

> *And what is your frame of mind toward others?* Are you in harmony with everyone—by willing one thing? Or are you divisively in a faction, or are you at loggerheads with everyone and everyone with you? Do you want for everyone what you want for yourself, or do you want the highest for yourself, for yourself and for yours, or that you and yours shall be highest? Do you do to others what you want others to do to you—by willing one thing? This willing is the eternal order that orders everything, that brings you into harmony with the dead and with the people you never saw, with

---

[4] Kierkegaard, *The Sickness unto Death*, 123.

[5] Kierkegaard, *Upbuilding Discourses in Various Spirits* (Princeton: Princeton University Press, 1993) 129.

> strange people whose language and customs you do not know, with all the people on the whole earth, who are blood relatives and eternally related to divinity by eternity's task to will one thing.[6]

Kierkegaard quite clearly argues in this portion of the text that the "alliances" and "crowds" that people form in their attempt to evade becoming single individuals are always factional; they are always rejections of an ethical stance toward the "universally human."

(3) In Kierkegaard's main ethical treatise, *Works of Love*, he paints two pictures: (a) how human beings act when they are defiantly remaining psychologically immature, and (b) how human beings act when they are open to growth in the direction of becoming genuine individuals. He describes these possibilities under the headings of "preferential love" and "divine love"—that love that flows out of hearing the command: "You shall love your neighbor as yourself." Preferential love means loving those who are similar to us, those we like, those who feed and reinforce our native egoism. Commanded divine love is love for all human beings without partiality and without expecting gain for ourselves. He refers to the parable of the Good Samaritan as a key example, noting that Jesus turned around the lawyer's question by asking "Which one of these three proved to be a neighbor?"[7] Those who are open to psychological growth act as neighbors to others, and at the same time they recognize all other human beings as neighbors to them. In other words, the category *neighbor* comes into existence in response to the divine command, and it has both subjective and objective facets. Under the regime of preferential love, the *neighbor* cannot truly exist; there are only friends and enemies.

I have outlined the heart of Kierkegaard's anthropological vision; I transition now into a closer comparison with Girard's vision. As with "gospel parallels" books, we can place passages from the two authors next to each other and see how close they were in many of their core ideas.

---

[6] Kierkegaard, *Upbuilding Discourses in Various Spirits*, 144.

[7] Søren Kierkegaard, *Works of Love* (Princeton: Princeton University Press, 1995) 22.

*Mimetic Desire*

The phrase most commonly connected with Girard's psychology is "mimetic desire;" Kierkegaard did not use the Danish equivalent of that phrase, but it is clear that he saw the same phenomenon in human behavior and culture. He used the Danish word *Sammenligning*, for example, which is translated into English as "comparison," but when the context in which he uses it is examined carefully, it is clear that he means that sort of comparison of oneself with others that is one aspect of the behavior of human beings under the regime of psychological immaturity. It is a looking around at others with envy because one lacks a psychological and spiritual unity within oneself. Kierkegaard often employed parables to illustrate his message, and one of the more memorable is the parable of the worried lily. A common lily lived among assorted other flowers and plants. One day, a bird came along and told the lily that in another place there were beautiful Crown Imperial Lilies that were much more impressive. The worried lily asked the bird to peck away the soil around its roots and carry it away to the place where the more beautiful lilies lived. "Alas, on the way the lily withered" and died. Kierkegaard explains the parable: "The lily is the human being. The naughty little bird is the restless mentality of comparison (*Sammenligning*), which roams far and wide, fitfully and capriciously, and gleans the morbid knowledge of diversity; and just as the bird did not put itself in the lily's place, comparison does the same thing by either putting the human being in someone else's place or putting someone else in his place."[8] In our state of immaturity, we are thin, insubstantial selves, living on the horizontal plane of social expectations and fashions. We are blown here and there by the winds of the crowd, the mass, the horde of similarly insubstantial selves that surround us:

> It indeed seems as if in order to begin to be oneself, a human being first of all must be furnished with what the others are and by that find out then what he himself is—in order then to be that. But if he falls into the snare of this optical illusion, he will never become himself....From "the others" a person of course actually finds out only what the others are—it is in this way that the world wants to deceive a person out of becoming himself. "The others" in turn do not know what they themselves are either but continually know only what "the others" are.[9]

[8] Kierkegaard, *Upbuilding Discourses in Various Spirits*, 169.

[9] Kierkegaard, *Christian Discourses* (Princeton: Princeton University Press, 1997) 39–40. See Girard, *Deceit, Desire, and the Novel* (Baltimore: Johns Hopkins University Press, 1965) 16: "Subjectivisms and objectivisms, romanticisms and realisms, individual-

Kierkegaard's message in this discourse is that it is through the vertical relationship with God that a person finds his or her true sense of self, meaning, purpose, contentment in life; "one cannot be oneself merely by being before others" on the horizontal plane. Compare this passage in Girard:

> When modern theorists envisage man as a being who knows what he wants, or who at least possesses an 'unconscious' that knows for him, they may simply have failed to perceive the domain in which human uncertainty is most extreme. Once his basic needs are satisfied (indeed, sometimes even before), man is subject to intense desires, though he may not know precisely for what. The reason is that he desires *being*, something he himself lacks and which some other person seems to possess. The subject thus looks to that other person to inform him of what he should desire in order to acquire that being. If the model, who is apparently already endowed with superior being, desires some object, that object must surely be capable of conferring an even greater plenitude of being.[10]

This passage leads me to assert that summaries of Girard's thought should begin with the concept of *lack*, not with the concept of *mimetic desire*, because it is this sense of lack that is the deep existential root of the phenomenon of acquisitive mimesis. This passage from *Things Hidden since the Foundation of the World* is also exactly on point:

> René Girard: No one can see that the true nature of violence is deduced with implacable logic, from the simple and single rule of the Kingdom. No one can see that disobeying or obeying this rule gives rise to two kingdoms which cannot communicate with one another, since they are separated by a real abyss. Mankind can cross this abyss, but to do so all men together should adopt the single rule of the Kingdom of God. The decision to do so must come from each individual *separately*, however; for once, others are not involved.
>
> Jean-Michel Oughourlian: If we follow your reasoning, the real human subject can only come out of the rule of the Kingdom; apart from this rule, there is never anything but mimetism and the 'interdividual.' Until this happens, the only subject is the mimetic structure.
>
> René Girard: That is quite right....[11]

---

isms and scientisms...all defend the same illusion of autonomy to which modern man is passionately devoted."

[10] Girard, *Violence and the Sacred* (Baltimore: Johns Hopkins University Press, 1977) 145–46.

[11] Rene Girard, *Things Hidden since the Foundation of the World* (Stanford: Stanford University Press, 1987) 199.

"Interdividuality" is a term coined by Girard that indicates a psychological state of social entanglement that is so thorough that it entails a *lack* of selfhood, a *deficiency* of genuine subjectivity and self-awareness. The same message is communicated very clearly by Kierkegaard:

> ...as an individual you are eternally obliged to make an accounting of your opinion, of your judgment. And in eternity you will not be pryingly and busily asked, as by a journalist, whether there were a great many who had the same—wrong opinion, but only whether you had it; whether you have pamperingly accustomed your soul to judge light-mindedly and unthinkingly along with the others because the crowd judged unthinkingly; whether you perhaps have corrupted the better part in you by boasting along with the crowd that you were many and that you were justified because you were many, that is, you were many who were wrong.[12]

*The Crowd Is Untruth*

In Girard's essay "The First Stone," he contrasts the miracle worker Apollonius of Tyana, who spurs a crowd to stone to death a beggar, with Jesus, who saves the woman caught in adultery from being stoned to death. Girard says that after the crowd disperses one by one, beginning with the eldest, "Instead of the mindless uniformity of the mob, we watch genuine individuals emerging from the crowd. The Gospel text can be read almost allegorically, as the emergence of genuine personhood out of the primordial mob."[13] This echoes precisely the repeated theme in Kierkegaard that the gospel message disperses the violent crowd and leads human beings to become individuals before God. The two authors are calling attention to the link between hypocritical self-righteousness and the violence of crowds.

Kierkegaard wrote an important essay on this theme: "the crowd is untruth."[14] He begins with the observation that there is "a view of life which holds that where the crowd is, the truth is also"; there is another view however, "which holds that wherever the crowd is, there is untruth." A crowd, he argues, is in its very concept untruth, regardless of whether it consists of "the lowly or the nobles" because it "renders the single individual wholly unrepentant and irresponsible." No one, as an individual, would have the courage to walk up to Christ and spit on him, but "since they remain in a crowd, they have the courage for it—what frightening untruth."

---

[12] Kierkegaard, *Upbuilding Discourses in Various Spirits*, 132.

[13] Girard, "The First Stone," *Renascence* 52, no. 1 (1999) 14.

[14] I am using my own translation, which is chapter one above. In the Princeton series of Kierkegaard's Writings, it is in volume 22, *The Point of View*, 105–112.

"The crowd is untruth. There is therefore no one who has more contempt for what it is to be a human being than those who make it their profession to lead the crowd...For to win a crowd is not so great a trick; one only needs some talent, a certain dose of untruth and a little acquaintance with the human passions." When I read these words, I cannot help but to see them as a prophetic anticipation of Adolf Hitler and his rallies. On this subject, Gabriel Rossatti makes this perceptive comment: "Both Kierkegaard and Arendt comprehended, following Socrates, that *de-individualized* individuals whose habitat is modernity become liable to the commitment not only of 'radical evil,' but rather of 'infinite evil;' for, as Arendt discovered through Eichmann, 'the greatest evil perpetrated is the evil committed by nobodies, that is, human beings who refuse to be persons.'"[15] I recall also, with agreement, a statement I heard once from Bruce Kirmmse, one of the leading Kierkegaard scholars, who said that he viewed Kierkegaard as the most anti-fascist thinker in the modern world. The "witness for the truth," Kierkegaard continues, will "talk with each privately, on the streets and lanes—to split up the crowd, or to talk to it, not to form a crowd, but so that one or another individual might go home from the assembly and become a single individual." The untruth that inheres in the existence of the crowd is that it excludes God and the "neighbor" in the sense of the divine command to love the neighbor as oneself. The crowd thus cannot recognize genuine human equality; "every one who is really aware," Kierkegaard says, "that the task is to love the neighbor, he is also aware of what human equality is."

*"If we had lived in the days of our fathers..."*

For Girard, one of the most important passages in the gospels is found in Matthew 23 and its parallel in Luke 11. This passage is the "woe to you Pharisees!" speech in which Jesus calls the Pharisees and lawyers hypocrites and blind guides, and says that they build the tombs of the prophets who were killed by their ancestors. To their claim that they would not have taken part in killing the prophets, Jesus replies that this very claim shows that they are just like their ancestors. He is implying that the self-righteousness of the claim reveals the mentality that supports violence; this is a clear echo of the incident with the woman caught in adultery. Girard comments:

---

[15] See Gabriel Guedes Rossatti, "Kierkegaard, Hannah Arendt and the Advent of the 'Hollow Men' or towards a Kierkegaardian Reading of Eichmann in Jerusalem," in *Kierkegaard Studies Yearbook* 2014, edited by Heiko Schulz (Berlin: De Gruyter, 2014) 328.

> Now it is the Christians who say: *If we had lived in the days of our Jewish fathers, we would not have taken part with them in shedding the blood of Jesus.* If the people whom Jesus addresses and who do not listen to him fulfill the measure of their fathers, then the Christians who believe themselves justified in denouncing these same people in order to exculpate themselves are fulfilling a measure that is already full to overflowing. They claim to be governed by the text that reveals the process of misunderstanding, and yet they repeat that misunderstanding. With their eyes fixed on the text, they do once again what the text condemns.[16]

Kierkegaard presents a similar message:

> By means of an illusion a living generation often feels that it dares to pass judgment on a past generation because it failed to understand the good person—and itself becomes guilty of the same thing with regard to a contemporary. And yet it is in relation to the contemporary that a person must demonstrate whether he has the view of the moment or of the eternal. Afterward it is easy to decorate the graves of the noble ones and say, "If they had only lived now!"—now, just when we are in the process of doing the same thing to a contemporary.[17]

In Kierkegaard's critique of Christendom toward the end of his life, he focused on this same text in his important essay: "What Christ Judges of Official Christianity." He suggested that pastors in Denmark should be required to read this passage from the gospel aloud from the pulpit, stand silently for five minutes, and then sit down.[18] He comments:

> At the root of "Christendom" is the truth: the human being is a born hypocrite. The Christianity of the New Testament was the truth. But people sagaciously and knavishly invented a new kind of Christianity, one that builds the tombs of the prophets and adorns the graves of the righteous and says: If we had lived in the days of our fathers. And this is what Christ calls blood-guilt.
>
> What Christianity wants is: imitation. What the human being does not want is to suffer, least of all the kind of suffering that is authentically Christian, to suffer at the hands of people. So he discards imitation and thereby suffering, the distinctly Christian suffering. Then he builds the tombs of the prophets—that is one thing. And then he lies to God, to himself, to others, and says that he is better than those who put the

[16] Girard, *Things Hidden*, 175.

[17] Kierkegaard, *Upbuilding Discourses in Various Spirits*, 90–91.

[18] Kierkegaard, *The Moment and Late Writings* (Princeton: Princeton University Press) 132.

> prophets to death—that is the next. Hypocrisy first and hypocrisy last—and according to Christ's judgment: blood-guilt.[19]

Kierkegaard had come to the same view of Christian history that Girard would later articulate in the terms of his own theory:

> Thanks to the sacrificial reading it has been possible for what we call Christendom to exist for fifteen or twenty centuries; that is to say, a culture has existed that is based, like all cultures (at least up to a certain point) on the mythological forms engendered by the founding mechanism. Paradoxically, in the sacrificial reading the Christian text itself provides the basis. Mankind relies upon a misunderstanding of the text that explicitly reveals the founding mechanism to re-establish cultural forms which remain sacrificial and to engender a society that, by virtue of this misunderstanding, takes its place in the sequence of all other cultures, still clinging to the sacrificial vision that the Gospel rejects.[20]

The Anabaptist tradition has taken a similar stance, criticizing the complicity of the so-called Christian West in violence, ever since the sixteenth century. That tradition, however, has lacked the psychological and sociological sophistication of Kierkegaard and Girard, which is needed to move from ethical critique to anthropological critique. It is worth noting that Anabaptist scholars today are fascinated by Girard's thought, and that Kierkegaard was interpreted by Vernard Eller as thinking in tune with the Anabaptist worldview.[21]

### *Kierkegaard on Violence*

While most readers of Kierkegaard focus on philosophical or theological ideas in his writings, it is actually the case that Kierkegaard was also a psychologist and a sociologist before those disciplines were formally included in the fields of higher education. He was intensely interested in the phenomenon of violence, focusing on the beating and crucifixion of Christ; like Girard, he saw that episode not as unique in human history but as representative of violence more generally. In *Two Ages*, for example, he recounts witnessing a street fight in Copenhagen in which three men were ganging up against a lone victim; a crowd formed, and became indignant about the mismatch; the crowd then beat up the three assailants. Kierkegaard tried to

---

[19] Kierkegaard, *The Moment and Late Writings*, 135–36.

[20] Girard, *Things Hidden*, 181.

[21] See Willard M. Swartley, ed., *Violence Renounced: René Girard, Biblical Studies, and Peacemaking* (Telford, Pa.: Pandora Press, 2000) and Vernard Eller, *Kierkegaard and Radical Discipleship: A New Perspective* (Princeton: Princeton University Press, 1968).

explain to one of the avengers the irony in the situation, but he had no success.[22]

Girard focuses on the arbitrariness of the selection of the sacrificial victim. The scapegoat may have characteristics that set him or her apart, such as being a twin, walking with a limp, being a foreigner, and so forth, yet in a particular act of scapegoating the choice of victim is arbitrary, in that one foreigner may be killed while another is spared, for no apparent reason. The psychological need of the crowd is for a victim, *any* victim, such as Apollonius' hapless beggar. Kierkegaard's theory of violence, on the other hand, because of its theological orientation, sees those who mediate the divine call to spiritual growth as the victims who most clearly reveal the deepest motivations of human violence. The Prophets, Christ, and St. Stephen the protomartyr, are paradigmatic here; in our age: Gandhi, Martin Luther King, Jr., and Oscar Romero. Consider this passage from Kierkegaard's journals:

> How Did It Happen That Christ Was Put to Death?
>
> I can answer this in such a way that with the same answer I show what Christianity is.
>
> What is "spirit"? (And Christ is indeed spirit, his religion is of the spirit.) Spirit is: to live as if dead (to die to the world).
>
> So far removed is this mode of existence from the natural man that it is quite literally worse for him than simply dying.
>
> The natural man can tolerate it for an hour when it is introduced very guardedly at the distance of the imagination—yes, then it even pleases him. But if it is moved any closer to him, so close that it is presented in dead earnestness as a demand upon him, then the self-preservation instinct of the natural life is aroused to such an extent that it becomes a regular fury, as happens through drinking, or as they say, a *furor uterinus*.

---

[22] Kierkegaard, *Two Ages* (Princeton: Princeton University Press, 1978) 86–87: "I once witnessed a fight in which three men shamefully mistreated a fourth. The crowd watched with indignation; their hostile muttering began to stir them to action: some of the crowd converged on one of the assailants and threw him down, etc. The avengers thereby exemplified the same law as the assailants. If I may be permitted to interject my own incidental person, I will finish the story. I approached one of the avengers and attempted to explain dialectically the inconsistency of their behavior, but apparently it was quite impossible for him to engage in anything like that, and he merely repeated: 'He had it coming. Such a scoundrel deserves three against one.' This borders on the comic...."

> In this state of derangement he demands the death of the man of spirit or rushes upon him to slay him.[23]

Those who mediate the divine call to spiritual growth are singled out as recipients of the rage of fallen human beings who are in a state of mutiny against the call of redemption.

Famous leaders such as Gandhi and Martin Luther King Jr. are targeted, but also less famous persons if they criticize a crowd intent on violence. Moderate Hutus were killed in Rwanda in 1994, for example, if they did not support the massacre of Tutsis. Those who sought peace within the context of ethnic and political tensions in Indonesia were sometimes assassinated. Tawfik Hamid recounts how his efforts to escape from the jihadist group he had been drawn into in Egypt led to an effort to literally stone him to death.[24]

Is Kierkegaard's theory of violence only useful in explaining these special cases of killing the messenger? I think not, for the following reason. The deep fabric of Kierkegaard's understanding of violence works with the idea that human selves are immature, but we have the possibility of becoming more mature. There is our current "self" in its small-mindedness and immaturity, and our potential future self in its expanded openness to growth. The deepest root of violence is that our current self does not want to die to itself and undergo the possibility of conversion. Our current self "sees" the possible future self as a threat to be fended off; thus we must expend our psychological energy continually fighting against becoming an other to ourself, dying and being reborn as a changed self. We "know not what we do" in the sense that this drama that is happening deep within our souls is inaccessible to us. We act, without being fully aware of what we are doing, fending off our own possible growth by transforming other human beings into phantom

---

[23] Kierkegaard, *Søren Kierkegaard's Journals and Papers*, translated by Howard and Edna Hong (Bloomington: Indiana University Press, 1967–1978) 4: 4360.

[24] See Philip Gourevitch, *We Wish to Inform You That Tomorrow We Will Be Killed with Our Families: Stories from Rwanda* (New York: Farrar Straus and Giroux, 1998) 95: "Genocide, after all, in an exercise in community building"; Asna Husin, "Islamic Peace Education: Changing Hearts and Minds," in *Crescent and Dove: Peace and Conflict Resolution in Islam*, edited by Qamar-Ul Huda (Washington, D.C.: United States Institute of Peace Press, 2010) 152: "...voices of moderation, reason, and peaceful resolution of conflict were being silenced by coercive or violent means, including assassination, torture, and extortion"; Tawfik Hamid, *Inside Jihad* (Mountain Lake Park, Md.: Mountain Lake Press, 2015) 53: "Once, I gave a sermon at a local mosque, and after prayers a gang of radical Muslims confronted me and my dear friend Dr. Tarek Ragab. They punched him, and as we ran from the mob, they pelted us with stones."

images of the more mature self that we are called to become and deflecting onto them our anger at the pressure that self places on us.[25] The self does not want to become an other to itself, and this is played out in the world through attacks on other selves. God is calling us to live more fully into the *imago Dei*, which entails truly loving God and our neighbor as ourself; we reject this call by hating and killing our neighbors. We cannot reach God to silence the call of creation, so we do what we can; we lay violent hands on other human beings who are created in the image of God. This is Kierkegaard's deep theory of violence, and it works to explain violent acts in general, as well as suicide, and the "killing the messenger" form of violence (which reveals the psychological dynamics most clearly).

*Mass Shootings*

There is by now a long list a mass shootings in the United States in recent years, to say nothing of those in other parts of the world: Columbine High School, Virginia Tech University, Sandy Hook Elementary, Charleston church, San Bernardino workplace, Orlando nightclub, Las Vegas concert, Sutherland Springs church, Parkland Springs High School. This is only a partial listing, of course, but it serves to point to a phenomenon that Girard's thought seems, at first glance, ill-prepared to comprehend. He focuses on the classic scene of the lynch mob, the crowd that forges a tenuous unanimity through killing an individual or a small number of people. But in these mass shootings the dynamic seems to be turned upside down. Now it is the individual attacking a crowd rather than vice versa. The technology of the rapid-fire gun facilitates this possibility in the modern world in a way that was not possible in earlier centuries, of course, but this by itself does not explain the *why*; how is this phenomenon to be comprehended psychologically?

In Girard's thought, Satan plays a key role. For him, Satan is an event more than a person; Satan is the event of immoral, psychologically unhinged violence. So we can say of these mass shootings that they are instances when individuals become lightning rods for the event of demonic violence. Given that "normal" society is organized, unconsciously, around the avoidance of a war of all against all through acts of immoral violence, we can say that the violent actors in these situations are revealing through their actions the texture of violence that forms the fabric of society. This is not an awareness that

[25] I am summarizing, very briefly, my argument in *The Genealogy of Violence: Reflections on Creation, Freedom, and Evil* (New York: Oxford University Press, 2001); see page 67, for example.

"normal," law-abiding citizens can absorb, however, so the knee-jerk self-righteousness of human beings will label the killers as "monsters" who are "mentally ill." That they are signs of the "mental illness" or what Girard calls the "ontological sickness" of society in general is not a thought that can be thought.

Kierkegaard's perspective points out the obvious, from a theological point of view. These individuals who acted in this way had as their intention the killing of other human beings. There is at the root of the experience of sin and despair a rage against God and the call of God to grow spiritually. Since we cannot reach God to kill God and silence the voice that calls us, we opt for plan B, killing our fellow human beings who are created in the image of God and whom we are called to love as we love ourselves. The human self in utter despair is rejecting the call to love God, self, and neighbor; this leads to homicide, suicide, and a transcendental rage that can never reach its target. For Kierkegaard, the crowd is untruth, but this understanding is always premised on the awareness that the crowd is untruth because it is made up of individuals who are in themselves living the untruth of flight from God.

### *Against Martyrdom*

Kierkegaard wrote an essay on martyrdom that is appropriate to consider at this point: "Does a Human Being Have a Right to Let Himself Be Put to Death for the Truth?"[26] One might assume that Kierkegaard's argument would be a defense of Christian martyrdom, using the *imitatio Christi* as the main motif. The reader is surprised, however, to find that the argument is quite different, and it actually answers the title question with a No. Jesus Christ was the one true martyr, because he was in his own being the Truth, and he could not be otherwise. He was Love, and in this violent world "love is hated." But Christians today are not Christ. We are sinners, Kierkegaard argues, and thus we cannot posit an ontological difference between ourselves and those who would violently abuse us. In obedience to the command to love the neighbor, we ought to be concerned for the neighbor's welfare, which entails avoiding putting ourselves in situations in which the neighbor becomes guilty of the crime of murder. Christians should not only be nonviolent and live in response to the Sermon on the Mount's call to "love the enemy";[27] they should also seek, as much as possible, to defuse the possibility of others becoming violent as well. In Kierkegaard's words:

---

[26] Kierkegaard, *Without Authority* (Princeton: Princeton University Press, 1997) 51–89.

[27] Kierkegaard, *Works of Love*, 67–68.

> The untruth consists in this, that the one struggling in this way relates himself to the others only polemically, thinking only of himself, not lovingly considering their cause. But in that case he is very far from being truly superior to them or superior in truth, because superiority is to be the counsel for the defense of one's enemy and as such to be concerned and, with more insight than he has, to keep watch so that he does not falsely become more guilty than he deserves.[28]

The phrase "to be the counsel for the defense of one's enemy" is reminiscent of Girard's statement that the Paraclete, the Holy Spirit, is the defense attorney, the one who seeks to defend human beings against the accusations of Satan, the prosecuting attorney.[29] In this case it is not the victims who are in need of defense, but the victimizers. Kierkegaard's argument leads us to realize that even the violent are in need of a Paraclete because they "know not what they do," because they are victims of their socialization into a violent crowd.

*The Epistemology of Love*

A key aspect of Girard's message in *Things Hidden* is the concept of the "epistemology of love":

> Love is at one and the same time the divine being and the basis of any real knowledge. The New Testament contains what amounts to a genuine epistemology of love, the principle of which is clearly formulated in the first Epistle of John: "He who loves his brother abides in the light, and in it there is no cause for stumbling. But he who hates his brother is in the darkness and walks in the darkness, and does not know where he is going, because the darkness has blinded his eyes." (1 John 2:10–11) . . . Love is the only true revelatory power because it escapes from, and strictly limits, the spirit of revenge and recrimination that still characterizes the revelation in our own world, a world in which we can turn that spirit into a weapon against our own doubles, as Nietzsche also showed.[30]

Similar thoughts were articulated by Kierkegaard. The passage "God is love" from the first Epistle of John was one of his favorite passages; he commented on it again and again.[31] He understood Christ to be the incarnation of God's love for humanity, and to thus be the key to human self-

---

[28] Kierkegaard, *Without Authority*, 88.

[29] Girard, *The Scapegoat* (Baltimore: Johns Hopkins University Press, 1986) 207.

[30] Girard, *Things Hidden*, 277.

[31] Some examples: Kierkegaard, *Upbuilding Discourses in Various Spirits*, 269–74; *Works of Love*, 121, 278–79; *Christian Discourses*, 84; *The Moment and Late Writings*, 423.

understanding, the criterion for what it is to be a human person.[32] There is a memorable passage in *Practice in Christianity*, for example, in which he asks his reader to imagine a parent showing a child a series of pictures of notable figures from history such as William Tell and Napoleon. Slipped among the pictures there is an image of Christ on the cross, and the child is told that this was a form of punishment reserved for the worst criminals. The child asks what crime this man committed, and the parent says that "this crucified man was the most loving person who ever lived."[33] The message that is supposed to be impressed upon the child is that in this fallen world "love is hated," a phrase that Kierkegaard employed repeatedly.[34]

*Kierkegaard has Girard Surrounded*

In my opinion, "Kierkegaard has Girard surrounded." I mean by this that Girard's thought tends to limit itself to the horizontal plane of social relations, in the wake of the human fall into sin. Kierkegaard's thought provides us with deeper reflections on what it means to fall into sin, particularly in *The Concept of Anxiety* and *The Sickness unto Death*; and it also provides us with much more extensive reflections on conversion, spiritual growth, and ethics (in works such as "Purity of Heart Is to Will One Thing" and *Works of Love*). Girard's thought tends to avoid making ethical arguments, so that his readers are left to work out the ethical implications of his thought on their own. In Kierkegaard, I argue, there is a rich treatment of the many different aspects of philosophical and theological anthropology and ethics, not simply an intense focus on the horizontal plane of social psychology. Kierkegaard's thought as a whole subtly employs an "oscillating fan" vision of human existence. We are born into and socialized within a horizontal plane, a violent crowd of some sort. We are called to disentangle ourselves from that crowd and rise up into genuine selfhood and subjectivity. This rising up allows us to be vertically related to God, and thus to truly hear the commandment, the "royal Law": "You shall love your neighbor as yourself."[35] We are then sent back down from the vertical to the horizontal, as changed agents who are able to be agents of change in the world. Girard's thought is sometimes described as a "phenomenology of redemption," but it is my contention that

[32] Kierkegaard, *The Sickness unto Death*, 113–14.

[33] Kierkegaard, *Practice in Christianity*, 175.

[34] Kierkegaard, *Works of Love*, 120; *Practice in Christianity*, 197–98; *For Self-Examination* (Princeton: Princeton University Press, 1990) 84.

[35] Kierkegaard, *Works of Love*, 24.

the phenomenology in Kierkegaard is actually much richer and more up-building for the reader.

Paolo Diego Bubbio provides an intriguing angle on this topic by arguing that Girard's comments on the divinity of Christ are actually an alternative form of the ontological argument for the existence of God. Instead of "God is that, the greater than which cannot be conceived," Girard is proposing the idea that Jesus Christ is the One, without whom we could not understand our violence as human beings.[36] Left to our own devices and our own epistemologies, we human beings will always rationalize our violence, and never gain the ability to critique it and experience an exodus from it. That exodus requires the entry into history of God; this is precisely what the doctrine of the divinity of Christ expresses, according to Girard: "Violence is the controlling agent in every form of mythic or cultural structure, and Christ is the only agent who is capable of escaping from these structures and freeing us from their dominance."[37] In Kierkegaard we find the same idea. Christ is the true human being precisely because he is God incarnate; he is the Prototype, the model for true love of neighbor and the one who accomplishes that revelation from above without which we would never come to see our despair and how it leads to violence. This is the message of *Works of Love* and *The Sickness unto Death.*

As an example of the idea that Kierkegaard provides a richer phenomenology of redemption than does Girard, consider this passage from *Practice in Christianity*:

> Thus what can be said to *draw to itself* must first and foremost be something in itself or must be a something that is in itself. That which is not in itself cannot possibly draw to *itself*. But this certainly is the case with the sensate, the secular, the momentary, the multiple—in itself it is nothing, is empty. In the last resort, it cannot be said to draw to itself; it can only deceive. . . .
>
> What truly can be said to draw to itself must be something higher, more noble, which draws the lower to itself—that is, truly to draw to itself is to draw upward, not to draw downward....

[36] Bubbio, *Intellectual Sacrifice and Other Mimetic Paradoxes* (East Lansing: Michigan State University Press, 2018) 115–28.

[37] Girard, *Things Hidden*, 219.

> ... when that which is to be drawn is in itself a self, then truly to draw to itself means first to help it truly to become itself in order then to draw it to itself, or it means in and through drawing it to itself to help it become itself.—Therefore, truly to draw to itself means something twofold—first to make the self, which is to be drawn to itself, to be itself, in order then to draw it to itself....
>
> So, then, what truly can be said to draw to itself must be something in itself or something that is in itself. So it is when truth draws to itself, for truth is in itself, is in and for itself—and Christ is the truth. It must be the higher that draws the lower to itself—just as when Christ, the infinitely highest one, true God and true man, from on high will draw all to himself. But the human being of whom this discourse speaks is in himself a self. Therefore Christ also first and foremost wants to help every human being to become a self, requires this of him first and foremost, requires that he, by repenting, become a self, in order then to draw him to himself. He wants to draw the human being to himself, but in order truly to draw him to himself he wants to draw him only as a free being to himself, that is, through a choice.[38]

For Kierkegaard, the Creator is always seeking to give genuine selfhood to human beings through the event of psychological and spiritual maturation; but we cannot receive this gift as long as we remain outside of ourselves, living mimetically in the crowd. This event of becoming truly human, gaining true subjectivity, is the heart of lived Christian faith.[39] This is the message of both Kierkegaard and Girard, but it is my contention that Girard's authorship lacks the fullness of articulation that Kierkegaard gives to this idea in *Upbuilding Discourses in Various Spirits*, *Works of Love*, *Christian Discourses*, *Practice in Christianity*, *For Self-Examination*, and *Judge for Yourself!*, books that I have only been able to scratch the surface of in this essay.

### *Insight into Violence Comes from Above*

I have been noting some differences between Kierkegaard and Girard, but there is one point at which they are clearly in agreement, and it is a very important point. Whenever there is a mass shooting or a terrorist attack of some sort, the press immediately begins to search for the "motives" of the violent agents. They look for online posts or verbal statements of support for certain groups or ideologies, as recounted by friends or family members.

---

[38] Kierkegaard, *Practice in Christianity*, 158–60.

[39] Kierkegaard, *Practice in Christianity*, 206: "The truth is within me, that is, when I am truly within myself (not untruthfully outside myself)...."

Books written by scholars, such as Mark Juergensmeyer's *Terror in the Mind of God: The Global Rise of Religious Violence*, take a similar approach, in that the search for motives relies on discovering the thoughts that were in the minds of the violent agents. Juergensmeyer travels the world to interview terrorists and their supporters. This may seem to be flippant way of putting it, but Kierkegaard and Girard, at a very deep level, are not interested in such thoughts, because a Christian interpretation of violence takes as its starting point a particular verse in the Bible: "Father, forgive them, for they know not what they do" (Luke 23:34). Girard comments:

> Does the idea of the unconscious belong to the Gospels?...The sentence that defines the unconscious persecutor lies at the very heart of the Passion story in the Gospel of Luke: "Father, forgive them..." In this passage we are given the first definition of the unconscious in human history, that from which all the others originate and develop in weaker form.[40]

Kierkegaard, in *The Sickness unto Death*, analyses the various forms of "despair," psychological malformation, as a condition of which the despairing person is unconscious. The ideas in the heads of violent people are, in the final analysis, the ravings of the morally insane, and a deep and truthful diagnosis of the situation is not going to come from the insane people themselves. The source of true insight is always transcendent; it is a *revelation* from above. This is the basic presupposition of Kierkegaard and Girard, and it stands as a profound critique of the assumption that is at work whenever people think that access to "motives" requires nothing more than awareness of the conscious thoughts or ideologies of those who are violent.

### *Conversion*

Jean-Michel Oughourlian sums up well the sense in which Girard is a theorist of conversion:

> If I understand you properly, today there can be no real knowledge of mimetic desire and its victimage mechanisms without shattering what in each of us is still structured or is always trying to restructure itself in accordance with this desire and these mechanisms. That means that the awareness we have sought from the beginning of these discussions is only truly accessible through an experience similar to what has traditionally been called religious *conversion*, though there may be no reason to avoid describing it in rational terms at the same time.[41]

---

[40]Girard, The Scapegoat, 110–11.

[41] Girard, *Things Hidden*, 400.

The central message of Girard's *Deceit, Desire, and the Novel* is that conversion is necessary for human beings to gain an ability to see their entanglement in the web of mimetic desire. Girard's interpretation of history maintains that certain key verses in the Bible are the engine driving a slow, subtle, unseen-but-nevertheless-powerful, epistemological conversion of humanity over more than two millennia. We now cannot avoid seeing the world through the lens of concern for victims. Conversion is also at the core of Kierkegaard's vision and message, as we have seen, and he is drawing on precisely the same biblical tradition.

We have noted that there are many key ideas in these two authors that are so similar as to be almost identical. Girard only rarely referred to Kierkegaard in his writings, but those references do indicate a positive attitude of general agreement.[42] Tracing the influence of one thinker on another is not always an easy task, but we can say with confidence that if Girard had explicitly turned his attention to Kierkegaard as he was writing *Deceit, Desire, and the Novel*, the Danish author could have been a sixth major voice included in that book. Kierkegaard, while not a "novelist" in exactly the same sense as Dostoevsky, was a writer of "novelistic" philosophical works, an anthropological theorist, and a theologian who shed light on the dynamics of conversion. Kierkegaard saw the same entanglement of human beings with others on the horizontal plane that Girard came to call "mimetic desire," and he offered profound reflections on the phenomenon of violence that can and ought to be brought into conversation with Girard's reflections.

[42] See Deceit, *Desire, and the Novel*, 58; *The Scapegoat*, 173; *To Double Business Bound* (Baltimore: The Johns Hopkins University Press,1978) 26–27; *The Girard Reader* (New York: Crossroad, 1996) 268; *Evolution and Conversion: Dialogues on the Origin of Culture* (New York: T & T Clark, 2007) 111; *Mimesis and Theory: Essays on Literature and Criticism*, 1953-2005 (Stanford: Stanford University Press, 2008) 115, 145, 158; and p. xi of Girard's Foreword to Robert Hamerton-Kelly, *The Gospel and the Sacred: Poetics of Violence in Mark* (Minneapolis: Fortress Press, 1994): "Mimetic theory is too realistic and commonsensical to be confused with one more nihilistic stepchild of German idealism. And yet, unlike the positivistic social sciences, it is not blind to paradox; it can articulate the intricacies of human relations just as effectively as a Kierkegaard or a Dostoevsky."

### *Kierkegaard and Girard as Trojan Horse Apologists*

The sense in which Girard wrote as a Christian apologist has been treated at length by Grant Kaplan and also discussed by Paolo Diego Bubbio.[43] According to Bubbio's description of "right Girardians," for whom the religious grounding of his thought is essential, and "left Girardians," who feel comfortable stripping Girard's thought of its religious elements and treating it as an agnostic sociological theory,[44] I clearly belong to the first group. I view the heart of Girard's thought as unveiling the drama of human history as a struggle between Satan and the Holy Spirit, and the notion that such a paradigm could be "secularized" strikes me as ludicrous.[45] To bolster my position, I can refer to an intriguing passage in *Evolution and Conversion* in which Girard's interviewers quote a passage from something that I had written that is exactly on point, namely:

> Girard ought to drop the pretense of adhering to the methodological atheism of social science, which has decreed that religious postulates are unacceptable foundations for understanding human behavior. He ought to write straightforwardly as a Christian apologist and argue that a theological mode of knowing is required for real insight into human behavior.[46]

Girard's response to this quotation is fascinating:

> ...the approach to facts in the social sciences should be devoid of both religious and anti-religious assumptions....If you postulate the *a priori* truth of religion from the start, your reasoning would have a far weaker apologetic value. The mimetic theory has an apologetic value in terms of Christianity *only* if you assume all the restrictions of knowledge of the scientific attitude.[47]

This admission on his part opens up another way of interpreting his authorship as a whole.

---

[43]Kaplan, *René Girard, Unlikely Apologist: Mimetic Theory and Fundamental Theology* (University of Notre Dame Press, 2016).

[44] Bubbio, *Intellectual Sacrifice*, 202.

[45] See, for example, the last two chapters of *The Scapegoat*, which bear the titles: "Satan Divided against Himself" and "History and the Paraclete."

[46] Bellinger, *The Genealogy of Violence*, 88.

[47] Girard, with Pierpaolo Antonello and João Cezar de Castro Rocha, *Evolution and Conversion: Dialogues on the Origin of Culture* (New York: T & T Clark, 2007) 150.

*Deceit, Desire, and the Novel*, which focused on the phenomenon of mimetic desire, was a work of literary criticism that did address religious themes, particularly in Dostoevsky, but the central ideas in the book fit in well in the world of academic literary discourse in general, where there is little discussion of religion or theology. *Violence and the Sacred*, likewise, was a work that laid out the bridge between mimetic desire and scapegoating, but it did so in the language of academic anthropology and psychology. The last paragraph of that book says that modern Westerners have managed to "extricate" themselves from the sacred and have lost the memory of "generative violence," but this is a blindness that creates a crisis; Girard describes his own task in addressing this crisis as exposing "to the light of reason the role played by violence in human society." Note that Girard does not say that his task is to speak theologically about the ongoing role of violence in cultural formation.

Those who are familiar with Girard's life story know that during that phase of his life that led up to the writing of *Deceit, Desire, and the Novel* he underwent a profound religious conversion, and gained a new sense of commitment to the Catholic faith in which he had been raised by his pious mother. This commitment only strengthened as the years passed, and he was a very active member of his local Catholic parish, even serving as a lay eucharistic minister. The quote above suggests that Girard saw his theory as having an apologetic goal, but he had decided that the most effective way to reach that goal was to consciously suppress theological language, if it would be seen as setting an *a priori* agenda. He decided to play along with the language game of modern academia, which places "restrictions" on the forms of speech that are acceptable in a "scientific" age. But his intention all along was to advance the cause of mimetic theory as a kind of Trojan Horse that would lead eventually to a time in the future when the truth of the gospel message could be conveyed more openly and directly. These comments in *Battling to the End* round out the picture: "All of my books have been written from a Christian perspective. My conversion is what put me on the mimetic path and the discovery of the mimetic principle is what converted me. It is unreasonable to say that my first two books are two halves of a whole (because I was relatively discreet about Christian revelation in them) and that all the others should be tossed out. Yet this attitude is quite common."[48]

[48] Girard, *Battling to the End* (East Lansing: Michigan State University Press, 2010) 196.

Stephen Jay Gould uses the phrase "non-overlapping magisteria" to refer to the realms of science and religion.[49] He has in mind the natural sciences, but in the social sciences, the notion that there could be a "non-overlapping" relation between sociology and theology is not plausible in the long run. This is the truth on which the notion that Girard's theory is "secular" runs aground. *Things Hidden since the Foundation of the World* presented the biblical roots of his insights into scapegoating, which he had already conceptualized as he was writing *Violence and the Sacred*, but decided to hold in reserve. In *The Scapegoat* he summarizes the theory of scapegoating in the first half of the book, followed by commentaries on the New Testament and Christian history in the second half. In *I See Satan Fall Like Lightning* this message is amplified, and Nietzsche and Nazism are presented as the "escalation to the extreme" of human rebellion against the truth of the gospel message. *Battling to the End* is a meditation on apocalyptic themes, echoing the last book of the New Testament. The late Girard writes, in sum, from the perspective of a Christian apologist who has gained a hearing in the academic world precisely because his earlier Trojan Horse strategy worked. But it is my contention that his theory was always theological, all the way down. Girard's anthropology is derived from the Bible, and it makes no sense to say that a biblical anthropology is non-theological.

The case for Kierkegaard as an apologist is obviously less ambiguous than that of Girard, but a parallel can still be drawn. Large swaths of the secondary literature on Kierkegaard written in the twentieth century adopt a stance that is similar to that of the "left Girardians." The religious elements of his thought are downplayed, as he is compared and contrasted with Kant, Nietzsche, Heidegger, Sartre, and others. He is labeled "the father of existentialism," whatever that is supposed to mean. But a case can be made that Kierkegaard's "first authorship," which spans the works from *Either/Or* to the *Concluding Unscientific Postscript*, is a rough parallel with Girard's *Deceit* and *Violence and the Sacred*, in the sense that he was establishing his reputation as a thinker in the world of academic discourse. Later, he wrote more forthrightly and clearly as a Christian author. He was attempting to "introduce Christianity again—into Christendom"[50] just as Girard was trying to do in his explicitly Christian works: "In effect, this sacrificial concept of divinity must 'die,' and with it the whole apparatus of historical Christianity, for the Gospels to be able to rise again in our midst, not looking like a

[49] Gould, *Rocks of Ages: Science and Religion in the Fullness of Life* (New York: Ballantine Books, 2002).

[50] Kierkegaard, *The Point of View*, 42.

corpse that we have exhumed, but revealed as the newest, finest, liveliest and truest thing that we have ever set eyes upon."[51] Kierkegaard also sought to critique the "apparatus of historical Christianity" so that a truthful articulation of what it means to be a follower of Christ could be made. This is the central theme of the books that make up the last phase of his authorship.

My thesis is that Kierkegaard and Girard are like two modern evangelists, each giving his own perspective on the gospel story. There are other evangelists as well: Fyodor Dostoevsky, Karl Barth, Hans Urs von Balthasar, Dietrich Bonhoeffer, Simone Weil, C.S. Lewis, and so forth, but the two I have been discussing provide the deepest insights into the psychological roots of violence.

[51] Girard, *Things Hidden*, 235–36.

# 4

# Kierkegaard
## Copernicus of the Spirit

"The people who walked in darkness have seen a great light." These words from Isaiah 9:2 can fittingly be applied to the cumulative effect of the writings of the great early modern astronomers Nicolaus Copernicus (1473–1543), Johannes Kepler (1571–1630), and Galileo Galilei (1564–1642). In the Middle Ages, the members of European society, from the least to the most educated, lived in the dark with regard to certain basic truths about the shape of the earth and the motion of the planets—truths that are now common knowledge for school children all over the world.

Copernicus was able to imagine that the planets are actually spheres revolving around the Sun, even as they rotate around their own axes. He realized that this scenario effectively accounts for the various appearances offered by phenomena in the heavens and on the earth. The seasons, for example, could now be understood by combining the idea that the earth's axis is tilted, with the idea of yearly transit around the Sun, placing the Northern hemisphere closer to the Sun in the Summer. Around 1510, when these concepts were coming into focus in Copernicus' mind, they were radical and bizarre. A heliocentric perception of the cosmos was such a major upheaval for customary thought that Copernicus was most likely wise to delay the publication of the full version of his theory until 1543, the year in which he died.

Kepler developed Copernicus' insights further by discovering certain laws of planetary motion that explained even more precisely the data provided by astronomical observations. He realized that the orbits of the planets were not perfect circles but ellipses and he was able to specify certain mathematical relationships involved in arcs, areas, and orbits. Kepler's added insights revealed a dynamic universe in which the Sun is actively moving the planets around in their orbits.

Galileo is perhaps the best known of these three astronomers because of the Church's dramatic proceedings against him. He continued to refine and develop the insights of his predecessors regarding inertia, parabolic trajectories, and other basic laws of motion. He was a major force in transforming the study of nature from a qualitative, philosophical enterprise into a quantitative, mathematical, and experimental process. He also used a homemade telescope to confirm and develop Copernicus' view of the solar system by seeing that there were moons orbiting Jupiter. It was this activity in particular that got him into hot water with the authorities. Defenders of the traditional Ptolemaic worldview rightly saw the developing heliocentric astronomy as a fundamental threat to their belief system. Galileo was tried and convicted of heresy in 1642. He was allowed to "recant" his views and live out the rest of his life under house arrest. He has become a symbol of the honest seeker after truth who is persecuted by fearful and small-minded authorities. In an expression of popular culture such as the song "Galileo" by the Indigo Girls, the singers "call on the resting soul of galileo king of night vision king of insight." In 1992 he was officially pardoned by the Vatican.

To describe the intellectual situation before these astronomers as "darkness" is a metaphor with substantial weight. Those who think that they understand the world correctly when they are actually misconstruing it in fundamental ways are truly in the dark. They cannot see the world in which they are living clearly. They are living in a fog—a veil of illusions generated by their own minds. They have naively accepted their own perceptions of the world as correct interpretations of the nature of things. The light that shines upon them reveals their anthropocentrism and its inadequacy as a basis for thought. What is needed for a clear perception of reality is a way of seeing that is not trapped by naïve egocentricity—one that allows for a higher, transcendent point of view.

The irony of this situation is clear to us now. When the Inquisition placed Galileo on trial, the Inquisitors thought that they were defending the Christian tradition against the appearance of new and heretical ideas that presaged a departure from faith and the advent of secularism. In hindsight, we can see that it was Copernicus, Kepler, and Galileo who were truly opening the door that leads into a higher, theocentric way of perceiving reality, as opposed to the naïve view that was truly anthropocentric and thus secular.

The central idea that I hope to communicate in this chapter is that we are today walking in a kind of darkness that is analogous to the darkness of the Middle Ages—the darkness of violence. Violence itself, as the reality of human evil, is a form of moral and spiritual darkness, and it is doubly compounded by the intellectual darkness apparent in the fact that we do not understand why we are violent. We human beings not only do evil things, but we are also ignorant about why we do them. This is the case with all of us, from the least to the most educated, though there are certain exceptions to this generalization.

Recall some event of violence that was the lead story on the evening television news within the last ten years. Almost inevitably, a reporter will be speaking with a school principal, or a mayor, or a pastor, or a grieving parent, and they will say something like "We don't understand why senseless acts of violence like this happen." They are speaking quite truly when they say that. Or think of an article in a major news magazine discussing such an event and perhaps even going beyond mere reportage to attempt some sort of explanation or consideration of what this event teaches us about "human propensities for evil." If you have ever read such an article and found it unsatisfying and unenlightening you know the nature of the problem. And if we rise above the level of the masses to consider the writings of psychologists, philosophers, historians, and so forth, who have reflected on these questions, we are likely to find more self-confidence, but also a bewildering variety of explanations of violence that point in many different directions. This variety, which is helpfully charted in a book such as *Explaining Hitler* by Ron Rosenbaum, reveals another dimension of the intellectual darkness that envelops us. If even those brilliant minds who have reflected on human violence for years cannot progress beyond the scenario of the blind men and their elephant, then the true dimensions of the problem begin to loom even larger.

It is my view that our modern age is not entirely lacking in authors who are similar to Copernicus, Kepler, and Galileo. Just as these light bringers performed their service in revealing the shape of the outer world, we also have light bringers in the task of understanding our inner world, our spirit and its malformations. In this context I will consider Søren Kierkegaard, Karl Barth (1886–1968), and René Girard.

Kierkegaard was widely read in the twentieth century, but it is far from clear that he was widely understood. In most cases, his interpreters and critics laid over his writings a heavy layer of their own biases, preoccupations, and jargon. This resulted in a phenomenon that I refer to as Kierkegaard Graffiti. Just as the vandal who spray paints a building hastily and then runs away has no real appreciation for the architecture of the building he is defacing, so also did Kierkegaard's deep and complex authorship become the victim of misconstrual and slander by people who did not expend the time and effort required for developing a clear understanding of his central concerns. Just one example of this graffiti is the phrase "the leap of faith" which is considered by many authors of encyclopedia articles to be the perfect summary of "Kierkegaard's philosophy." It turns out that he never used that phrase in his writings, and far from being an adequate summary, it is actually an incoherent and uneducated piece of disinformation.[1]

A more accurate summary of Kierkegaard would proceed along these lines. Kierkegaard understood the world as the sphere of the creative activity of God. He took very seriously the fundamental biblical theme that God creates the universe through speech. Everything that exists does so because God is speaking it into existence. The human soul is that unique place in all of nature where the voice of God can be heard and responded to consciously. The animals, vegetables, and minerals are simply given from God's hand; but human beings are able to be aware of their divine source. We are not only spoken into existence, but we also have the ability to be hearers of that speech. This is our transcendent nobility as human beings, but it is also our peril.

Just as we are superior to the lower animals because we can respond to our Creator consciously, so also can we sink below them into the abyss of sin. The psychology of the animals is set, determined. But our psychology is rooted in freedom. Another way of putting this is to say that we do not simply exist; we are coming into existence. Our character is not set in stone; our character is shaped by our experiences, our fears and anxieties, our relationships with other people and with our Creator. We have the ability to shape our own character (and to be shaped) through our response to the voice of creation that is speaking us.

The fact that we are not determined means that we can experience an emotion that is unique to us: angst. Angst arises out of the ambiguity of our future. There are various possibilities open to us if we choose to allow our self to develop in this direction or that direction. The most basic choice which presents itself to us at all times concerns our response to the divine call of creation. We can respond positively to this call and allow ourselves to be drawn forward into the fullness of selfhood that God intends for us, or we can attempt to deafen ourselves to God's voice and seize control of our selfhood. This is precisely what Adam and Eve did, and what we all do as their children. They sought to "become as God," to usurp the place of God as the shaper of their future. In the same way, human beings down through the centuries have tried to manage and contain their angst by turning away from God in an attempt to avoid the pain of personal growth. We find it easier to reinforce the status quo of our souls and our societies than to allow the continuing process of creation to make, unmake, and remake us.

---

[1] See Alastair McKinnon, "Kierkegaard and the 'Leap of Faith,'" *Kierkegaardiana* 16 (1993): 107–25.

When we start down this path of deafening ourselves to the voice of God, we quickly develop a psychological inertia. Our commitment to avoiding the pain of growth is so strong that we organize our character and our societies around that commitment. When we cut ourselves off from the fullness of what the future could hold for us, we inevitably become dwarfed, stunted, and misshapen as persons. Instead of living creatively in the tensions of existence before God (freedom and necessity, the eternal and the temporal), we careen in one direction or the other, seeking then to fortify ourselves within one of those poles of existence. What we are seeking to evade above all else is the possibility that we could actually become ourselves before God. Instead of moving in faith into the fullness of life that God calls us to, we choose to follow the pathway that Kierkegaard calls "the sickness unto death."

When God comes to us in the person of Christ, what do we do? We could allow him to heal us of our sickness and lead us back into the process of creation. But we don't do that. We are enraged by the voice that judges our smallness and choice of mediocrity. We must silence this voice in order to protect ourselves from its disturbing call. We stop up our ears and rush upon him to kill him.[2] Kierkegaard is pointing us in the direction we must look if we seek to understand the violence that erupts from the depths of human soul. Violence is not "senseless"; it has a purpose. It seeks to fend off the possibility that always lies before us—the possibility that we could become the mature, loving human beings that God wants us to be.

In the preceding paragraphs I have drawn on themes found in Kierkegaard's books *The Concept of Anxiety*, *The Sickness unto Death*, and *Works of Love* along with thoughts expressed elsewhere in his writings. I will return to Kierkegaard again toward the end of this chapter, but I turn now to the other two authors I am comparing with Kepler and Galileo.

Karl Barth's theological vision arose out of his reflections on the killing fields of World War I. He was appalled by how easily the progressive Protestant culture in which he had been educated became a culture of death and destruction on a huge scale. Many of his favorite professors, who had spoken eloquently about the gradual development of the kingdom of God on earth and the advance of Christian civilization had suddenly become militaristic warmongers. He realized that "something was rotten in Denmark." The problem was Europe's vague, nominal, cultural Christianity that Kierkegaard had attacked so vehemently at the end of his life. Barth's commentary on Romans picked up where Kierkegaard's attack left off, blasting and

[2] Kierkegaard, *Søren Kierkegaard's Journals and Papers*, 4: 4360.

exposing the illusion of a triumphantly advancing Christian world in Europe. Barth was avidly reading Dostoevsky and Kierkegaard at this time, and the influence of the Danish thinker upon Barth continued to be strong throughout his career.

When Nazism came to the forefront in Germany in the 1930s, Barth was well prepared to theologically analyze and denounce it in the Barmen Declaration and other writings. He realized that the illusion of Christendom had been dissolved, leaving in its wake a revival of neopaganism that was animated by a hatred of the divine revelation that had been communicated through the experience of the Jewish people, Jesus Christ, and the apostles.

At the heart of Barth's mature thought as a theologian we find a clear echo of the central theme in Kierkegaard: God's speech that brings us into being. The structure of the *Church Dogmatics* is built upon the foundation of "The Doctrine of the Word of God." God has spoken the creating and redeeming word through the prophets and the apostles, and God continues to speak to human beings in all times and places. Barth is careful to not allow the word of God to be understood as a frozen entity contained in the scriptures. God is living and speaking in the present moment in time. Reading the Bible opens up our hearing so that we can be awake to that living speech in our time and place.

Barth understands God as "the One who loves in freedom." God's love for us is not bound within any structure of metaphysical necessity. God's love for us is always greater than our ability to understand it or rebel against it. God's grace precedes us and comes after us. God's patience waits for us to end our self-imposed choice of flight and death. In the final analysis, evil in the universe can be nothing other than that which is opposed to God's grace; as such, it does not have a divine origin or a coherent and necessary place in God's providential ordering of life.

Barth was always a very politically oriented theologian. Toward the end of his life, he reflected on the Lord's Prayer: "Our Father who art in heaven, hallowed be thy name, thy kingdom come." In this context, he spoke of the root cause of human hatred and violence. When people act toward human beings more as wolves than as neighbors, it is due to a colossal ignorance of God, as God's nature is revealed through Christ. Ignorance of God works itself out in an ignorance of one's fellow human beings that expresses itself in caprice, hatred, rancor, and duplicity. If human beings truly knew God, then their relations with others would express faithfulness, love, and peace, just as God has reached out to us with precisely those attributes. When we see the neighbor as a creature of God, then we will live not against but with and for one another.[3]

René Girard is another light bringer in our world. I am comparing him to Galileo because he has made a great impact on the scholarly world through his writings and lectures. He has almost single-handedly turned the attention of thousands of scholars and thinkers to the task of reflecting on violence and the roots of human culture. He is a wide-ranging polymath who brings together in remarkable ways the study of modern European literature, ancient Greek tragedy, social science, and biblical studies. His comments on scapegoating, human sacrifice, lynch mobs, and related phenomena have been so thought-provoking that a huge literature of response has already come into existence, and many scholarly conferences have been held around the globe on his thought.

Girard begins with the concept of mimetic desire. We human beings have a natural tendency to look to others as models of success. We think that by imitating others we deem to be successful, we will come to share in their greater fullness of being. We want to have what they have so that we can be as important as they are. This basic driving force in human affairs, mimetic desire, can be seen in the psychology of small children, in advertising, in romantic relationships, in fashion, in economics, and on and on. But if I am copying the desires of others, wanting to possess what they possess, then by definition I will create a rivalry with those others for the possession of those things. And if those others are creating a rivalry with me, then we have the recipe for a war of all against all for possession of the idols of our desire.

How does human society prevent itself from degenerating into a chaos of violence driven by envy? "It is expedient that one should die for the sake of the many." The idea of channeling a society's violence toward a scapegoat is the solution to the problem. Killing a scapegoat, or attacking a minority group within society, provides an outlet valve for the build up of hatreds, resentments, and violent impulses that are generated by mimetic desire. Killing the scapegoat is a cathartic event that creates a new sense of social unanimity that did not exist before. Sacrifice becomes salvific for the society, and it becomes the cornerstone of both religion and culture.

But this answer to the problem is false because the problem should not exist in the first place. In other words, deceit becomes the one thing needful for society as it must not become aware of the injustice involved in its destruction of arbitrary scapegoats. Society must lie to itself about its founda-

[3] Karl Barth, *The Christian Life* (Grand Rapids: Eerdmans, 1981) 132.

tion, because the mimetic desire at the root of the social system is itself a falling away from God; Girard calls it an "ontological sickness."[4]

This is the point at which Girard's vision of human culture leads beyond the narrowness of secular social science to a broader theological anthropology. Girard clearly states that we can only articulate this understanding of human culture because our eyes have been opened up by the Bible. It is the cumulative effect of divine revelation in the Hebrew and Christian scriptures that has exposed the ontological sickness of mimetic desire and the scapegoating mechanism. The high point of revelation is the gospels' depiction of the crucifixion of Christ, which tears the mask off of culture's insistence that it is in the right when it executes people. The gospels expose this lie by clearly showing that Christ is innocent and that those who are killing him are in the wrong. In that revelation God triumphs and Satan is defeated. Girard understands Satan to be that principle in human psychology and culture that cries out for bloodshed, for violence, for revenge, for destruction.

Girard speaks primarily about a crowd attacking a scapegoat. In the news recently, we have heard about teenage boys walking into their high schools and turning them into shooting galleries, or Timothy McVeigh blowing up a federal building, or terrorists attacking buildings in New York City. In situations like this, an individual, or small group of individuals, is attacking a large crowd rather than the other way around. Girard's theory is not as helpful in understanding situations like this as it is in understanding the psychology of the lynch mob. This is the case because Girard's forte is social psychology, not individual psychology. I suggest that here Kierkegaard can take our understanding to a deeper and more fundamental level.

Aristotle said that "all action intends a good." In other words, whenever human beings act, they *think* (in some ambiguous sense of the word *think*) that they are doing something good. The Nazis thought they were making the world a better place by killing as many Jews as possible. President Truman thought he was ending World War II sooner by dropping atomic bombs on two Japanese cities. Timothy McVeigh thought he was striking a dramatic blow against a tyrannical federal government. In other words, human action is always either directly ethical in the eyes of the actors, or it is a kind of "teleological suspension of the ethical" that amounts to the same thing. McVeigh could admit that killing innocent people is not in itself a good thing, but the badness of the act is outweighed by the goodness of the prophetic statement. Similar thoughts run through the minds of Islamic ter-

[4] Girard, *Deceit, Desire, and the Novel*, 238–39.

rorists. And ironically, similar thoughts will no doubt run through the minds of those troops who carry out retaliatory actions against the terrorists. Everyone is innocent in their own eyes, because everyone is intending a good.

From Kierkegaard we can gain a better understanding of the phenomenon of human evil. From him we can learn that in the case of the most twisted psychologies the self is so filled with rage toward God and the ongoing process of creation that the person's actions no longer make any sense in terms of this world. I am thinking of how the Columbine shooters killed others and then committed suicide. They had already checked out of this world. Their actions can't even be described as selfish since they result in the death of the self. I am thinking here of the way we search in vain to find any shred of rationality in the actions of the World Trade Center terrorists. When terrorists cold-bloodedly board airplanes and suicidally guide them to a murderous apocalypse, their actions can aptly be described as expressing a "transcendental rage." The object of this rage is God. The human self has become so twisted and malformed that the only good it can aim at is the affirmation of the self in utter defiance of God and the goodness of creation. The self's desire to avoid the pain of growth is so strong that it has declared war on God and God's creatures, which includes the self itself. Thus we can understand the very close relationship between the suicidal mentality and the homicidal mentality. Ultimately, the most effective way for the self to prevent itself from growing psychologically is to end its own existence as a self.

It is sometimes said that self-righteousness is at the root of violence. This is true, and Kierkegaard, Barth, and Girard help us to develop a nuanced understanding of the truth at work here. The most basic root of violence is the self not wanting to become an other to itself, the self not wanting to die and be reborn in a more mature form. The self-righteousness that leads to violence is the attempt of the immature self to fortify itself in defiance of the call of creation. We insist that we are in the right in relation to others, because we want to be in the right in relation to God. We want to be as God, knowing good and evil, so that we can avoid the pain of creation.

H. Richard Niebuhr once said, "The cross in history may be compared to the kind of an event which an astronomer means when, having computed the positions of the planets with the aid of his excellent Ptolemaean wisdom he discovers a planet in a position that does not fit into the scheme. His whole wisdom is called into question, and eventually the Copernican or Einsteinian revolution of his science may result. So the cross as a simple event calls into question the foundations of our worldly wisdom."[5] From Kierkegaard, Barth, and Girard the full ramifications of this insight can be drawn out. From them we can learn to know the shape of the self, the mechanisms of fallen society, and the heart of the God who calls us all into a new world of grace and truth.

Songwriter Bruce Cockburn has written a song (Child of the Wind) which contains these words:

Little round planet in a big universe
Some times it looks blessed, some times it looks cursed
Depends on what you look at obviously
But even more it depends on the way that you see.

Kierkegaard, Barth, and Girard give us the way of seeing that we need if we are to understand human violence. But intellectual understanding by itself will not bring an end to violence. The end will only come when we human beings spiritually open ourselves up to God's love and allow God to bring us out of the darkness of transcendental rage and into the light of God's grace and peace, so that we can truly begin to love our neighbors as ourselves.

---

[5] H. Richard Niebuhr, *Theology, History, and Culture: Major Unpublished Writings* (New Haven: Yale University Press, 1996) 205.

# 5

# Kenneth Burke and the Theory of Scapegoating

Words sometimes play important roles in human history. I think, for example, of Martin Luther's use of the word *grace* to shatter Medieval Catholicism, or the use of *democracy* as a rallying cry for the American colonists in their split with England, or Karl Marx's vision of the *proletariat* as a class that would end all classes. More recently, *freedom* has been used as a mantra by those on the political left and the political right. If a president decides to go war, with the argument that *freedom* will be spread in the Middle East, then we are reminded once again of the power of words in shaping human actions. This is a notion upon which Kenneth Burke placed great stress as he painted a picture of human beings as word-intoxicated, symbol-using agents whose motives ought to be understood *logologically*, that is, from the perspective of our use and abuse of words.

In the following pages, I will argue that there is a key word that has the potential to make a large impact on human life in the future, the word *scapegoat*. This word is already in common use, of course, but I suggest that it is something akin to a ticking bomb in that it has untapped potential to change the way human beings think and act. This potential has two main aspects: 1) the ambiguity of the word as it is used in various contexts, and 2) the sense in which the word lies on the boundary between human self-consciousness and unself-consciousness. The first aspect is seen in the way the word scapegoat has been used with a positive connotation in theology ("Christ is the scapegoat who carries away sins") and with a negative connotation in other contexts ("X was made a scapegoat for the fall of Enron"). The second aspect refers to the phenomenon that scapegoating behavior may be occurring, but it could not be described as such by those who are behaving in that way. Hitler could not say to a crowd "We will use the Jews as scapegoats upon whom we are venting our frustrations!" If the word scapegoat were used with that degree of self-consciousness, then the behavior would be rendered impossible. From this it follows that if greater awareness of the importance of the word could be fostered and spread throughout society, the effect may be a limitation of human impulses toward violence.

In this essay I will discuss these issues by providing some brief comments on the usage of the word scapegoat in modern English, noting the ambiguity referred to above. This will set the stage for an extended look at Kenneth Burke's reflections on scapegoating, which offered a strong impetus to moving beyond simple usage of the word to a sophisticated philosophical analysis of the word as a key window into human behavior. Burke's thoughts on scapegoating, however, remained a bit scattered and unfocused, even though he recognized that the cluster of concepts guilt / victimage / catharsis "is the very centre of man's social motivation."[1] That Burke's reflections were powerful yet not fully developed leaves the door open for further refinement of the theory of scapegoating. Such refinement has been advanced already by René Girard, who was directly influenced by his reading of Burke, though he developed his own particular understanding of catharsis. In the conclusion of this chapter I will attempt to continue developing the theory of the scapegoat by placing Burke in a rhetorical parlor along with Girard, Eric Voegelin, and Ernest Becker.

### *A. The Word Scapegoat*

The English word scapegoat was coined by William Tyndale in his 1530 translation of Leviticus 16:8: "And Aaron cast lots over the two goats: one lot for the Lord, and another for a scapegoat" [spelling modernized]. The most common usage of "scapegoat" during the sixteenth through the eighteenth centuries is seen in theological interpretations of Christ's death on the cross as a substitute for sinners. John Asgill's *The Metamorphosis of Man, by the Death and Resurrection of Christ from the Dead* (1727) is representative of this genre:

> Man was freed from Sin before Christ was:
>
> For the Moment that the Sin of Man was laid upon the head of that Scape-Goat, Man was legally discharged from it.
>
> As soon as the Ram (Christ in a Figure) was caught in the Thicket, the whole Humanity (in the Type of Isaac) was let go.
>
> And therefore, when Christ was taken, there was not a Man taken with him: *I am Jesus of Nazareth whom ye seek, let these therefore go their way.*
>
> But the Sin of the whole Humanity, did from thence remain upon the Head of that Scape-Goat, (*He bare our Sins in his own Body upon the Tree*)

---

[1] Kenneth Burke, *Permanence and Change: An Anatomy of Purpose*, 2nd ed. Indianapolis: Bobbs-Merrill, 1965 [originally published in 1935] 285.

till he had carried them out of the Sight of God and Man, by the Sacrifice of himself.[2]

The idea that Christ on the cross took upon himself the sins of humanity as a substitute recipient of God's wrath and punishment is the most widely known interpretation of the theological meaning of Christ's death. For many Christians, this interpretation is the central idea upon which all Christian doctrine turns; for some non- or ex-Christians, who reject this idea as primitive thinking, it is indeed the essential Christian idea, which is why Christianity must be abandoned. Both of these groups might be surprised to learn that there are other interpretations of the death of Christ that were articulated in the history of Christian theology, most notably the ransom theory and the moral influence theory, which frame the interpretation of the cross in terms that do not rely on wrath and punishment at all. Nevertheless, theological texts such as Asgill's account for the bulk of the uses of the word scapegoat during the early modern period. At the same time, however, the second definition of the word was also present in various texts. This can be described as the *secular* usage, as seen in the following examples. From Bolingbroke's *Remarks on the History of England* (1780): "If the kingdom had escaped entire destruction in this forlorn condition, it must have been by miracle, and without any merit on the part of those, who govern'd; but this entire destruction would much more probably have follow'd, after a long series of calamities; without any other excuse on their part, than that of charging the catastrophe to the account of fortune, the common scapegoat of unskilful ministers."[3] Thomas Davies' *Memoirs of the Life of David Garrick* (1780) says this: "He had no inclination to become the scapegoat in this business; and he urged Mr. Garrick to perfect the articles of their agreement, by which it was covenanted, that neither of the contracting parties should accommodate matters with the patentee without a comprehension of the other."[4] A character in Mrs. Hannah Cowley's play *A School for Greybeards*

---

[2] John Asgill, *The Metamorphosis of Man, by the Death and Resurrection of Christ from the Dead*, Part I. London, 1727. Based on information from English Short Title Catalogue. Eighteenth Century Collections Online. Gale Group, 255.

[3] Henry St. John Bolingbroke Viscount. *Remarks on the History of England*. By the Right Honourable Henry St. John, Lord Viscount Bolingbroke. A new edition. London, 1780. Based on information from English Short Title Catalogue. Eighteenth Century Collections Online. Gale Group, 178.

[4] Thomas Davies, *Memoirs of the life of David Garrick, Esq. Interspersed with characters and anecdotes of his theatrical contemporaries. The whole forming a history of the stage, which includes a period of thirty-six years.* By Thomas Davies. ... Dublin, 1780. 2 vols.

(1787) says: "Upon my word—so I must be the scapegoat! But I won't be blamed I vow...."[5]

James Frazer's *The Golden Bough* was a summarizing survey of the anthropological knowledge that had been compiled during the nineteenth century. His section on "The Scapegoat" was published in 1913. He referred to phenomena in a variety of cultures, times, and places, that were similar to the scapegoat ritual mentioned in Leviticus. In some cases, the sins and diseases of the community were symbolically placed on an animal, such as a dog, chicken, goat, or monkey, which was then driven away or killed. In other cases, the scapegoat was a human being. Frazer presents, to mention just one example, an account from the Yoruba people of Africa, who would choose one member of the community once a year to be paraded through the area, symbolically collecting the sins of the people. He is then ceremonially beheaded, which is "a signal for joy, thanksgiving, and for drum beating and dancing, as an expression of their gratification because their sacrifice has been accepted, the divine wrath is appeased, and the prospect of prosperity or increased prosperity assured."[6]

Frazer's overall framework suggested a trajectory of progress from the magical superstitions of "primitive" peoples, to reflective religions, to the advanced scientific and secular knowledge of the modern West. This perspective is summarized well in his own words:

> The notion that we can transfer our guilt and sufferings to some other being who will bear them for us is familiar to the savage mind. It arises from a very obvious confusion between the physical and the mental, between the material and the immaterial. Because it is possible to shift a load of wood, stones, or what not, from our own back to the back of another, the savage fancies that it is equally possible to shift the burden of his pains and sorrows to another, who will suffer them in his stead. Upon this idea he acts, and the result is an endless number of very unamiable devices for palming off upon some one else the trouble which a man shrinks from bearing himself. In short, the principle of vicarious suffering

---

Based on information from English Short Title Catalogue. Eighteenth Century Collections Online. Gale Group, vol. 1, 60.

[5] Hannah Cowley, *A School for Greybeards; Or, the Mourning Bride: A Comedy, in Five Acts*. Dublin, 1787. Based on information from English Short Title Catalogue. Eighteenth Century Collections Online. Gale Group, 21.

[6] James Frazer, as quoted in John B. Vickery and J'nan M. Sellery, eds., *The Scapegoat: Ritual and Literature* (Boston: Houghton Mifflin, 1972) 11.

> is commonly understood and practiced by races who stand on a low level of social and intellectual culture.[7]

Frazer's condescending attitude toward the past has not stood the test of time very well, due partially to the fact that the twentieth century witnessed the unleashing of massive episodes of war and violence, such as Nazism, Stalinism, and the American atomic bombs. The moral and psychological superiority of modern Westerners over their *primitive* ancestors is difficult to maintain as an unquestioned assumption in the wake of such events. A plausible argument can be made that "magical" thinking is just as much present today as it ever has been, even though it may be invisible to those who think that they have escaped magic.

It is worth noting that the two uses of the word, the biblical/theological usage and the secular application of it, are discordant. It is assumed that when human beings are turning other human beings (or "fortune") into scapegoats they are doing something wrong, something unjust and improper. Blame is being placed on one person so that others may avoid facing the reality of their guilt honestly. But the biblical/theological usage describes the placing of blame on Christ as a positive thing for humanity, as the transcendent means of redemption. So, when God engages in scapegoating, blaming the innocent and letting the guilty go free, it is a good thing, but when human beings engage in scapegoating, it is an evil action. This discordance is noted here and will be taken up again toward the end of this essay.

### *B. Kenneth Burke on the Scapegoat*

The historical survey we have just completed paints the backdrop for a consideration of the contribution of Kenneth Burke to reflections on the scapegoat. It is my contention that Burke provided a very strong impetus toward the development of a more sophisticated understanding of the motives that drive scapegoating than had been articulated in the past. Burke deepens the discussion beyond the point to which Frazer brought it by asking the Why? question at a very deep level and providing us with thought-provoking answers.

Burke's *Permanence and Change*, published in 1935, included a subsection on "The Scapegoat as an Error in Interpretation." He refers to the desperate economic conditions of poor whites in the South, drawing an analogy with a psychological experiment. The experiment had shown that if one re-

[7] Frazer, quoted in Vickery, *The Scapegoat*, 3.

peatedly struck an iron bar to frighten an infant, while at the same time holding up a rabbit, then the infant would start to fear the image of the rabbit even when the bar was not present. Burke argues that the real cause of the suffering of poor whites was the economic structure of that time and place, but demagogues could easily suggest to them that the cause of their problems was black people: "the Negroes being the rabbit that is presented as the iron bar is violently struck, they take on the menacing quality of the bar…the Poor Whites adopt intimidation by lynching as the adequate solution to their problem."[8] For Burke, this is magical thinking and a case of "faulty means-selecting." His commentary in this section of *Permanence and Change* echoes Frazer's narratives in *The Golden Bough*. However, Burke warns against using the concept of scapegoating to designate "some special way of functioning not common to all men." Burke does not share Frazer's bias which sees modern, secular Westerners as qualitatively different from the *savages*. The trajectory of Burke's thought in the coming decades goes in the opposite direction, as it searches for the common structures underlying human behavior in all times and places. He will thus assume that if the *savages* sought to transfer their guilt to another and send it away, then *moderns* will have a secularized way of doing the same thing. Burke believed that we cannot escape from the history we are studying as easily as Frazer seemed to think we could.

*Permanence and Change* also includes an appendix "On Human Behavior, Considered Dramatistically." Burke argues there that the cluster of concepts guilt / victimage / catharsis / redemption "is the very centre of man's social motivation. And any scheme that shifts attention to other motivational areas is a costly error."[9] As a key example, he refers to the "Hitlerite emphasis," which puts "the stress upon a total cathartic *enemy* [the Jews] rather than upon the idea of a total cathartic *friend* [Christ]."[10]

Burke's analysis of Hitler was greatly expanded in his important review of *Mein Kampf*, published as "The Rhetoric of Hitler's 'Battle'" in *The Southern Review* in 1939.[11] This was a very substantive and insightful piece, comparable in philosophical quality to Eric Voegelin's *Die Politischen Religionen* [political religions] (1938), which also analyzed Nazism as an ersatz political

---

[8] Burke, *Permanence and Change*, 15.

[9] Burke, *Permanence and Change*, 15.

[10] Burke, *Permanence and Change*, 285.

[11] This was an expanded version of a speech given by Burke at the Third American Writers' Congress (1939). It was also collected in *The Philosophy of Literary Form* (1941).

theology.[12] Burke's concern was not simply to warn about the danger posed by Hitler, but also to prevent a similar fascist movement from gaining momentum in the United States. (Charles Coughlin, a Catholic Priest who addressed large Depression-era audiences with fiery quasi-fascist rhetoric, is an illustration of the atmosphere within which Burke was communicating.)

In "The Rhetoric of Hitler's 'Battle'" Burke emphasizes Hitler's strategy for motivating his audience: present to it an enemy that is cunning, ruthless, seductive, poisoning, corrupting, plotting, etc. If the masses have an object to hate that is *perfectly* evil, then the energy of their forward movement will be as powerful as possible. To paint a picture of reality in shades of gray, with ambiguities and guilt everywhere, is to dissipate energy. Democracy, the parliamentary, is another form of dissipation attacked by Hitler. The babel of voices in society leads to endless debate and inaction. There must be one strong voice inspiring the populace, creating communal spirit through rhetoric.

Burke presents Hitler as being very sensitive to the suffering that resulted from the Great War and the Depression. He sought to be a *doctor* who would give the German people the medicine they need to become well again:

> [a projection device is a] "curative" process that comes with the ability to hand over one's ills to a scapegoat, thereby getting purification by dissociation. This was especially medicinal, since the sense of frustration leads to a self-questioning. Hence if one can hand over his infirmities to a vessel, or "cause," outside the self, one can battle an external enemy instead of battling an enemy within. And the greater one's internal inadequacies, the greater amount of evils one can load upon the back of "the enemy."[13]

Burke places stress on Hitler as a kind of political theologian, a preacher who inverts the "hours of prayer" into "hours of vituperation." Hitler presented himself as a Prophet leading the people into an experience of new birth. He was also the Great High Priest who presided over the sacrificial machinery of death that was necessary for new life to come to fruition.

---

[12] Voegelin fled for his life to the U.S. shortly afterwards. My attempts to find primary or secondary connections between Burke and Voegelin have led to very little, which is puzzling given the similarities between the two authors as major contributors to twentieth century philosophical anthropology. The recent English translation of this work is here: *Modernity Without Restraint: The Political Religions, The New Science of Politics and Science, Politics, and Gnosticism*, edited with an introduction by Manfred Henningsen (Columbia: University of Missouri Press, 2000).

[13] Burke, *The Philosophy of Literary Form*, 202–03.

Burke concludes the essay by arguing that Hitler's main appeal was based on "a bastardization of fundamentally religious patterns of thought."[14]

During the next decade, with its momentous events, Burke wrote and published *A Grammar of Motives* (1945) and *A Rhetoric of Motives* (1950). In these two large books he continued to develop his understanding of scapegoating as a vital element of social formation. *A Grammar of Motives* contains a section on "The Dialectic of the Scapegoat." Burke articulates three key aspects of the *scapegoat mechanism*:

> (1) an original state of merger, in that the iniquities are shared by both the iniquitous and their chosen vessel; (2) a principle of division, in that the elements shared in common are being ritualistically alienated; (3) a new principle of merger, this time in the unification of those whose purified identity is defined in dialectical opposition to the sacrificial offering.[15]

Burke also points out in this section that the motivating impulse of violence is ambiguous in that it can be outwardly or inwardly directed. If it is possible to attack the scapegoat as an external object, then there is homicidal action; if such attack becomes frustrated, the violence can turn inward and become suicidal. Examples of this are seen in Germany's prolongation of World War II, even when it was clear that victory for them was impossible; the same was the case in Japan, and the image of a Japanese general committing ritual suicide as the allies close in is a perfect summarizing anecdote. If Burke were here today, he would no doubt have much to say about the merger of the homicidal and the suicidal motives in the 9/11 attacks.

The subsection on the scapegoat in the *Grammar* is important, but it is very short; the main substance of Burke's theory of scapegoating needs to be pulled together from other passages in the *Grammar*, *A Rhetoric of Motives*, *The Rhetoric of Religion*, and other essays. This has been done in a helpful way by William Rueckert in Chapter 4 of *Kenneth Burke and the Drama of Human Relations* and by Allen Carter in *Kenneth Burke and the Scapegoat Process*. The next several pages present a summary of their summaries. It needs to be noted however, that these summaries are in some ways easier to follow than Burke's writing itself. Burke's thoughts on scapegoating were scattered about in many different places in his writings. Though he acknowledged the centrality and immense importance of scapegoating, he

---

[14] Burke, *The Philosophy of Literary Form*, 219.

[15] Kenneth Burke, *A Grammar of Motives and a Rhetoric of Motives* (Cleveland: World Publishing, 1962) 406.

could not quite manage to write an essay on the topic that was both theoretically comprehensive and focused.

For Burke, the meaning of a word is not isolated. One cannot simply look up a dictionary definition of *scapegoat*, for example, and then be satisfied that one understands it. A word needs to be seen as part of a cluster or complex of terms, such as the negative, guilt, scapegoat, redemption, which is itself part of a larger philosophical interpretation of the human scene. In a cluster of terms, any one of them *logologically* implies all the others.[16] When this concept is grasped, then one is able to travel further down the road toward understanding than one could travel with the dictionary alone.

For Burke, there are seven key interlocked moments in the human drama: the negative, guilt, hierarchy, mortification, victimage, catharsis, and redemption. By *the negative* Burke means the moral prohibitions that are necessary to civilization: Thou shalt not lie, steal, kill, etc. This is one of the key elements of Burke's definition of man as a mark that distinguishes human beings from the lower animals.[17] The lower animals simply are what they are and do what they do; they are *positive*. But human beings can say No to each other and to themselves internally. Allen Carter gives a helpful anecdotal illustration of this point:

> I was in my backyard...from the other side of the fence came my neighbor's voice. Unaware of my presence, he was authoritatively laying down the law of his own turf to a visiting child: what to touch, what not to touch, where to go, where not to go, and so on. A few minutes later I caught myself telling my son not to kick his soccer ball onto Bermuda grass I had just watered. As I walked around the house, I heard my wife tell other children not to throw sand on the sidewalk she had just swept... *When we are initiated into language we are initiated into a system of commandments.*[18]

These are obviously mundane examples, but the nexus of commands and prohibitions within which all human beings are socialized in their vari-

---

[16] This point is expanded in Burke's *The Rhetoric of Religion: Studies in Logology* (Berkeley: University of California Press, 1970).

[17] "Man is: the symbol-using (symbol-making, symbol-misusing) animal, inventor of the negative (or moralized by the negative), separated from his natural condition by instruments of his own making, goaded by the spirit of hierarchy (or moved by the sense of order), and rotten with perfection." "Definition of Man," *The Hudson Review* 16, no. 4 (1963–64): 507. Reprinted in Language as *Symbolic Action: Essays on Life, Literature, and Method* (Berkeley: University of California Press, 1966) 16.

[18] C. Allen Carter, *Kenneth Burke and the Scapegoat Process* (Norman: University of Oklahoma Press, 1996) 56–57.

ous cultures cover all aspects of life, big and small. Because no one could ever perfectly internalize and obey all of these commandments, all human beings will feel guilt. We will all, at times, say things and do things that we shouldn't, causing harm to ourselves and others. We carry these feelings of failure and guilt inside of us, and we will seek some way to cleanse ourselves of those feelings.

But before I get to catharsis, I need to mention the concept of hierarchy. Every society will be constituted by a complex system of hierarchies.[19] Parents have authority over children, teachers instruct pupils, government officials enact laws that citizens must obey, religious leaders formulate doctrines that the faithful are expected to adhere to, the leaders of corporations give orders to the layers of their underlings, the rich employ the poor as servants, and so on. Society is stratified in many ways, and in some cases this becomes what Burke calls a *hierarchical psychosis*, such as the doctrine of White Supremacy. But even in relatively benign circumstances, the reality of hierarchical structures produces myriad forms of social divisions, frictions, resentments, and guilt feelings. The ideal of equal concern and affection of all human beings for all other human beings is a distant dream for fallen creatures who are entangled in complicated webs of hierarchy that were formed years, decades, or centuries before they were born. The spirit of hierarchy that shapes us thus produces it own set of guilt feelings regardless of where one finds oneself: "King and peasant are 'mysteries' to each other. Those 'Up' are guilty of not being 'Down,' those 'Down' are certainly guilty of not being 'Up.'"[20]

Mortification and victimage are the twin concepts that must be considered next. For Burke, the negative—the system of commands and prohibitions that makes civilization possible—is the bedrock of human psychology. When the force of the negative is primarily turned inwards, the result is mortification. In traditional language, this is asceticism and self-denial, which can take many different forms. Victimage occurs when the force of the negative is primarily turned outwards, as accusatory language directed toward other human beings. Others are vilified, demonized, condemned, and so forth, as a *projective* means of avoiding introspection and self-awareness. The extreme form of mortification is suicide; the extreme form of victimage is homicide. In Rueckert's words, "to make others suffer for our

[19] See Rueckert, *Kenneth Burke and the Drama of Human Relations*, 131–34.
[20] Burke, "Definition of Man," 506.

own sins is victimage; to make ourselves suffer for our own sins is mortification."[21]

For Burke, catharsis is one of the most important themes in literature and life. Human beings have a desire to be happy, but the burden of guilt that they carry within themselves is always working against happiness. There is thus a strong desire to be rid of the internal sense of guilt, pollution, pain, anxiety, and so forth. These hindering, debilitating emotions can be projected, mentally, onto an Other and sent away when that Other is expelled. This is the twentieth century psychological language that expresses the central concept of Leviticus 16. In Burke's words:

> The principle of drama is implicit in the idea of action, and the principle of victimage is implicit in the nature of drama. The negative helps radically to define the elements to be victimized. And inasmuch as substitution is a prime resource of symbol-systems, the conditions are set for catharsis by scapegoat (including the "natural" invitation to "project" upon the enemy any troublesome traits of our own that we would negate.) And the unresolved problems of "pride" that are intrinsic to privilege also bring the motive of hierarchy to bear here; for many kinds of guilt, resentment, and fear tend to cluster about the hierarchical psychosis, with its corresponding search for a sacrificial principle such as can become embodied in a political scapegoat.[22]

Catharsis through victimage makes possible a renewed sense of unity in the community of agents who are purifying themselves, and a renewed sense of personal happiness and peace. I think here of the chilling photographs of Nazis smiling and laughing in the midst of their work while nooses are hanging in the background or smoke is rising from chimneys.

Redemption is the last of the seven interlocked terms we have been considering.[23] This is the end product of the dramatic action of human culture. In the wake of the cathartic expulsion of guilt, evil, and decay, a social scene can be created that embodies the fellowship of the Good, the Righteous, the Victors, the People of God. This group defines itself over against the Other that represents evil, degradation, and guilt. That Hitler presented himself as a redeemer figure in this sense is clear, as Burke argues in "The Rhetoric of Hitler's Battle." But it is not just the obviously pathological characters who fit this description. Any political leader in any time and place will use rhetorical resources to articulate a vision of "redemption," "hope," "a new day for our nation," and so forth, with the goal of creating a more uni-

---

[21] Rueckert, *Kenneth Burke and the Drama of Human Relations*, 147.

[22] Burke, "Definition of Man," 510.

[23] See Rueckert, *Kenneth Burke and the Drama of Human Relations*, 131–34.

fied community in which the members of society will feel at peace with themselves as participants in a broader enterprise of human endeavor.

The overtly religious language used by Burke does not signify that he writes as a theologian or is promoting religion. It indicates that he believes that religion is not a private matter. Rather, culture is inherently religious and religion is inherently cultural. Burke, particularly toward the end of his writing career, sought to present a kind of secularized Christianity as a lens through which the human condition can and ought to be understood.[24]

Allen Carter helpfully summarizes Burke's complex understanding of the concept of scapegoating through three key metaphors: the rod, the ladder, and the skull.[25] *The rod* points to the sense of threat that attends not living within the boundaries laid out by the negative. If you disobey, you will suffer the consequences: If you break the law, you will be thrown in jail; if you slack off on the job, you will be fired; if you preach heresy, you will be excommunicated; if you make the wrong choice, you will regret it for the rest of your life. *The ladder* points to the hierarchical structures referred to above. Those structures create boundaries that can produce a sense of guilt if they are not maintained. Human beings also have a strong tendency to think of themselves as above other human beings who are shamefully below. *The skull* points to human mortality. Human beings realize, at least if they are being honest with themselves, that they are ephemeral and limited. The question of the meaning and ultimate purpose of life impacts people existentially and leads them to imagine what lies beyond the grave. Many aspects of human psychology can be interpreted along these lines as a struggle to understand one's life in the face of death.

In this section of the essay I have provided an overview summary of Burke's theory of the scapegoat. This is a very substantive theory that sought to integrate insights from literature, religion, and the social sciences to articulate an understanding of cultural dynamics. This was not an armchair exercise for Burke. He sought to address the catastrophic devastation of World War II. He was hoping that the writing of books and articles that increase human self-understanding could somehow mitigate human destructiveness. He saw clearly that one key distinguishing mark of human beings in relation to the lower animals is our ability to completely destroy ourselves and all of nature. If there is to be any possibility of "making the world a better place" through rhetoric, it would only be found when those who employ rhetoric to build a community do so with anthropological understanding.

---

[24] Rueckert, *Kenneth Burke and the Drama of Human Relations*, 127.

[25] Carter, *Kenneth Burke and the Scapegoat Process*, 3–27.

*C. Post-Burke Reflections on Scapegoating*

I turn now to consider a select group of authors whose reflections on violence can be placed together with Burke's in a rhetorical parlor: Eric Voegelin, Ernest Becker, and René Girard. Voegelin (1901-1985) was a political philosopher who wrote extensively on history, religion, and politics. He articulated a subtle theory of consciousness that grew out of his understanding of the key dimensions of reality as it is experienced by human beings:

> God and man, world and society form a primordial community of being. The community with its quaternarian structure is, and is not, a datum of human experience. It is a datum of experience in so far as it is known to man by virtue of his participation in the mystery of its being. It is not a datum of experience in so far as it is not given in the manner of an object of the external world but is knowable only from the perspective of participation in it.[26]

What he calls *world* in this passage he calls *nature* elsewhere. He is painting a picture of a vertical axis comprising God (transcendence) and nature (immanence), which is intersected by a horizontal plane of human sociality. *Man* (who can also be called the self, the person, the individual) is the locus of experience of the dimensions. This picture of reality is not unique to Voegelin; many other authors say similar things, including Kenneth Burke, who speaks of "four realms to which words may refer;" the natural, the socio-political, the logological (words about words), and the supernatural.[27] This corresponds well with Voegelin's scheme, with the caveat that Burke's analysis of humans as symbol using animals (logology) is similar to but not identical with Voegelin's analysis of the person's (man's) consciousness. (I have not found evidence that Voegelin read anything by Burke, or vice versa, but this makes the parallels between them more rather than less interesting, in my view.)

Voegelin's take on human violence and scapegoating arises out of his dimensional anthropology. For Voegelin, the ideal of human consciousness is balance and complexity. The mature person is one who is comfortable living in the middle of the vertical axis *in between* God and nature, with ethical concern for other human beings in society, and with an openness to psychological growth as a person on a journey through time. Unbalanced living is seen in the Gnostic who seeks to flee to a spiritual realm above nature. The

---

[26] Eric Voegelin, *Order and History, Volume 1: Israel and Revelation* (Baton Rouge: Louisiana State University Press, 1956) 1.

[27] Burke, *The Rhetoric of Religion*, 14–15.

opposite error is committed by a devotee of materialistic scientism who rejects the spiritual realm as illusory and claims that nature is all that is real. In the socio-political realm, the horizontal plane, pathological characters may become demagogic leaders who claim that the group is the highest value, in relation to which the individual is expendable. When rejection of the divine and the traditional structures of ethics are asserted by such leaders, the doorway is opened to mass killings that have as their goal the radical reshaping of reality in accordance with the dreams of the unbalanced leaders. The ancient Gnostic's flight from reality is transformed into the modern Gnostic's quest to reshape reality in his own narrow image.[28] Spiritual pathology and the political violence it entails arise out of a refusal to live within the complexity of reality in a balanced way.

Ernest Becker (1924–74) was a cultural anthropologist and philosopher whose writings paid a great deal of attention to human violence. His last two books, *The Denial of Death* and *Escape from Evil*, present an explanation of human behavior that focuses on fear of physical death. He claims that human beings commit acts of scapegoating because they believe that they can somehow, magically, transfer their mortality to others and kill that mortality by killing the others. The key to the puzzle of human behavior is "killing others in order to affirm our own life."[29] In the terms of Allen Carter's presentation of Burke, this is a version of *the skull* as a motive. Becker makes positive references to Burke, indicating that he is working in agreement with Burke's general argument. For example: "Burke was led to the central idea of victimage and redemption through Greek tragedy and Christianity; he saw that this fundamentally religious notion is a basic characteristic of any social order. Again we are brought back to our initial point that all culture is in essence sacred—*super*natural."[30] However, Becker's reduction of all human motives to one—fear of death—seems to indicate that Burke's attempt to introduce complexity into our understanding of human motives did not register well with Becker, who sought a simpler interpretation. It is the case that human awareness of mortality is an important factor in our psychology, but there are other factors not emphasized or even mentioned by Becker that are also important. In terms of Voegelin's analysis, Becker is combining the natural dimension (finitude) with the individual self's ability to envision its

[28] A helpful summary of Voegelin along these lines is provided by Glenn Hughes in "Balanced and Imbalanced Consciousness," in *The Politics of the Soul: Eric Voegelin on Religious Experience*, ed. Glenn Hughes (New York: Rowman & Littlefield, 1999) 163–83.

[29] Ernest Becker, *Escape from Evil* (New York: Free Press, 1975) 110.

[30] Becker, *Escape from Evil*, 115.

future. But the social plane as a motivating force does not come into focus for Becker in the way it does for the next author I will consider, Girard.

In my view, René Girard is the most substantive and influential voice working in the direct wake of Burke's reflections on scapegoating. Like Burke, Girard's thought centers on the fertile interface between literature and social science. From his reading of literature, particularly Shakespeare, Cervantes, Flaubert, Stendahl, and Dostoevsky, Girard articulated the theme of *mimetic desire*, which means that human beings copy the desires of others. Contrary to the modern myth of the autonomous self whose desires arise spontaneously from within, Girard suggests that the great writers reveal through their characters that human desires are most commonly shaped and directed by social contexts. We desire something, such as gold or an attractive potential mate, because we see others desiring that thing. But this is a recipe for conflict because if person A is copying the desire of person B for the possession of object C, then A and B will by definition become rivals to each other who are fighting for that thing. This behavior is easily observable in small children, but it is not a phase that human beings grow out of as they get older. The patterns of mimetic desire, rivalry, and conflict simply become much more sophisticated and convoluted. Girard argues that because mimetic desire is the basic structure of human psychology, we fall into a chaotic war of all against all. This situation can only be resolved through the *scapegoat mechanism*, a phrase he copies directly from Burke.[31] A society can focus its chaotic violence in a particular direction, toward a scapegoat, as a way of cathartically releasing its conflict and generating a new sense of unanimity and peace.

According to Allen Carter, "the Burkean self has neither firm foundation nor substance. A product of the verbal swirl, it is as insubstantial as a fading syllable, always already undergoing transformations made possible by the symbolic resources of language."[32] This concept parallels well Girard's idea that there is no autonomous self that precedes social relations. What we call selves are more like ghosts blown here and there by social winds of mimetic desire. But there is a key difference between Girard and Burke, which is articulated well by Carter:

[31] Burke, *Permanence and Change*, 14–17. "As for the scapegoat mechanism in its purest form, the use of a sacrificial receptacle for the ritual unburdening of one's sins, here also we can avoid the hypothetical introduction of a separate mental process."

[32] Carter, "Logology and Religion," 16.

> For Burke, what comes first is the system of commandments that proliferates and defines greater criminality. The language, being ethically charged, guides the behavior of its speakers but, perfecting its moral demands, induces in them guilt and the need for a surrogate victim. For Girard, all hands tend to mimic each other's reach for the same object, which leads to trouble and, in the end, to the establishment of the legal code. For Burke, legally induced guilt creates needs for self-justification that make it difficult for any reaching hand to consider compromise and withdrawal. For Girard, the scapegoat precedes the law. For Burke, the law precedes the scapegoat. Who is to say which should be privileged over the other? I am trying to suggest their doctrines are mutually reinforcing.[33]

This point could also be expressed through Burke's notion that in a cluster of terms the concepts mutually imply each other. It is not necessary, in other words, to ask whether the chicken came before the egg or vice versa.

At places in his books, Girard's thought takes a distinct turn in a theological direction, though he always says that he is not a theologian but an anthropologist. Girard claims that we are able to develop such a clear, conscious analysis of scapegoating precisely because of the biblical narratives. From the story of Cain and Abel to the account of Joseph unjustly imprisoned to the words of the Prophets to the passion accounts of the murder of Jesus, the Bible claims that truth is on the side of the victim, not on the side of the victimizers. This turns upside down the story that is always told by the scapegoaters, who justify their violence in their own eyes. The scapegoaters always claim that the one being killed is a guilty criminal who deserves to be punished. Girard argues that even though there are passages in the Bible that describe God in violent terms, the main trajectory of thought in the Bible points in the opposite direction. God is being progressively revealed as nonviolent, as peace and love.

---

[33] Allen Carter, "Logology and Religion: Kenneth Burke on the Metalinguistic Dimension of Language," *Journal of Religion* 72 (January 1992): 16.

*D. Synthesis*

We can combine the insights of these authors along these lines. The various dimensions of reality (God, nature, self, society) are regions within which human motives become focused.[34] They are "sovereignties" in the sense in which that term has been used recently by Jean Elshtain in her book *Sovereignty: God, State, and Self.* Because human beings tend to *fall* into more simplistic forms of thinking, rather than living with complexity, this means that patterns of scapegoating will develop that arise out of narrowly focused motives. 1) Those who see themselves as asserting God's sovereignty will act as judges of sinful humanity. This will take the form of an Inquisition, a Crusade, an attack by Muslim terrorists, or the bombing of an abortion clinic by a Christian fundamentalist. 2) Those who focus their motives primarily on the horizontal plane of culture and the state will reinforce their social unanimity through acts of scapegoating against an identified minority. The Hitlerite attack on the Jews, the Stalinist attack on counter-revolutionaries, the lynching of blacks in the deep South, and the massacre of Tutsis by Hutus in Rwanda, are examples of this. In the cases of Hitler and white supremacy, a vertical language of higher and lower races adds a naturalistic component to the rhetoric of horizontal scapegoating. In the Marx-influenced thought-world time predominates over essence, as the scapegoaters identify themselves with the ideal future and their victims with the corrupt past. 3) Those who see themselves as asserting the sovereignty of the self will seek to argue that the agent must be able to act in accordance with his or her purposes without any scenic interference. Individual autonomy must trump any laws which would restrict the self's freedom of choice. This passage from Burke illuminates this situation:

> [in the wake of Rousseau] we got a different notion of the individual: not the individual as an *integral* part of the popular whole, but the individual as a *divisive* part of the popular whole.

[34] Burke's comments on the structure of his "motivorum trilogy" are relevant here. Grammar relates to the vertical axis of ontology, substance; Rhetoric relates to the horizontal plane of community formation, Symbolic relates to the individual's identity. See "Identification and Consubstantiality" in *A Grammar of Motives and a Rhetoric of Motives*, 545–47. See also his section on "Order, the Secret, and the Kill" in *A Grammar of Motives and a Rhetoric of Motives*, 784–91. Order is "the ladder, cosmologized by the middle ages in what Lovejoy calls 'the Great Chain of Being.'" The Secret relates to the individual and the Symbolic. The Kill is social scapegoating. (789)

> Unheralded, even unnoticed, another "fall" had taken place. And instead of the individual as microcosmic replica of the popular macrocosm, we got the individual *against* the group.[35]

This picture we have just painted of the narrowing and fragmentation of human motives suggests the image of various limbs of a tree that can be climbed out on. One person climbs up vertically to be one with God's will; another person stresses group belonging as the highest priority; another claims that isolated selfhood trumps all else; another may seek to defend nature by joining an eco-terrorist cell. What is being evaded in all cases is the challenge of living in the center, the task of living at the intersection of the dimensions of reality in a way that holds them together in creative tension. When people climb out on a limb they are enacting the principle of *division, alienation*; as such they are inevitably going to see themselves as surrounded by *enemies* who have climbed out on other limbs. At that point, there is a strong likelihood that some form of war or scapegoating will occur. The specific forms of scapegoating may vary significantly from scene to scene, but the underlying dynamic will remain the same. Human conflict arises from our refusal to live in the center.

Put differently, human conflict arises from our refusal to become self-conscious. Scapegoating is the act of blaming others as a way of not facing clearly and honestly one's own guilt. Scapegoating is a flight from self-awareness. Thus when Jesus says on the cross, "Father, forgive them, for they know not what they do," he is bringing into articulation what Girard calls the *persecutory unconscious*. He says that in "this passage we are given the first definition of the unconscious in human history."[36] Those who are violent are not fully aware of what they are doing, and the violence has as its goal the maintenance of that unawareness. Thus, when thinkers such as those I have been considering pull back the veil to expose scapegoating they are working against the grain of human psychological sloth; they are working with the grain of authentic human maturity.

This statement summarizes Burke, Voegelin, Becker, and Girard, viewed synoptically. But we may also note a commonality between them in that they are all anthropological thinkers who are standing outside the fence of theology and looking in, commenting on what they see as the religious heart of human culture. By theology I mean the rhetoric of religion as it would be articulated by the preacher or the prophet who speaks from within the experience of faith, as opposed to the scholar who comments on it from

[35] Burke, *A Grammar of Motives*, 364.
[36] Girard, *The Scapegoat*, 111.

without. Of the writing of books and articles by scholars there will surely be no end, as they continually comment on each other's books and articles. The knowledge that is articulated in this way is sometimes very valuable. But if we ask how the human race is actually going to change, so that we "study war no more," I suggest that that possibility is only plausible if there are religious leaders, such as Martin Luther King Jr., who speak from within the experience of faith in a manner that constitutes a *public theology*. Scholars usually just communicate with other scholars and with students, but a religious leader, such as King or Gandhi, may be able to communicate with millions of people, speaking with a voice that draws from deep wells of religious tradition and political ideals.

I noted earlier the odd discordance in the two main uses of the concept of the scapegoat. When God scapegoats, it is good, but when human beings scapegoat, it is evil. Girard's thought wrestles deeply with this precise dilemma, which lies at the heart of Christianity as a theological system. Burke's contribution to this topic can be seen as an updated version of a projective psychological account of the origins of the idea of God. In other words, if human beings are symbol using and misusing animals, then there is a certain rationality to the act of inventing a God who employs scapegoating. By inventing such a God and worshipping and *obeying* him, human beings can claim that when they engage in victimage they are following God's lead and walking in the path of righteousness. If divine violence and wrath poured out on a victim is redemptive, then human wrath can also under the right circumstances be a microcosmic reflection of God's will and character. Burke's argument shows how this circular, self-reinforcing train of thought has its own rationality. But the other usage of the word scapegoat, which presumes the wrongness and inauthenticity of scapegoating, always seems to hang in the air as a sign of contradiction giving human beings an uneasy conscience. It is my suggestion that this other, so called *secular*, meaning of the word scapegoat has the potential to revolutionize theological worldviews by forcing us to consider what the world would look like if God was not in any sense involved in scapegoating. If a wrathful, scapegoating God who commands violence and enacts violence comes to be understood as a human invention, as a projection, then space is cleared for what Burke would call a *transubstantiation* of God.[37] The essence or substance of God could begin to be imagined as peaceful and loving. Or, in terms that would suit orthodox theology more comfortably, human beings could cease inventing or imagining God and allow their self-awareness to be impacted by a genuine revela-

[37] Burke, *A Grammar of Motives*, 320.

tion, a new theophany. "God is light, and in him is no darkness at all" (I John 1:5). The only sort of public theology that would be able to provide a decisive change in direction for humanity is one that decisively raised human self-consciousness to the awareness that there is no legitimate abuse of scapegoats, by either divine or human agents.

# 6

# Kenneth Burke's Anthropology and Ethics

## A.

Kenneth Burke is not known as an applied ethicist, in the sense that one would not usually think of his writings as a source of comments on particular ethical issues or dilemmas. He is not associated with an ethical theory either, in the sense that Kant is associated with deontology and Bentham with utilitarianism. But Burke's thought has a moral dimension, or is concerned with morality as an aspect of human life, as anyone who has read him is aware. The question is: How should we describe the relationship between Burke and ethics?

Let us consider Burke's pentad (agent, act, scene, agency, purpose, or who, what, where, how, why) as an illustration of the difficulty involved in this question. For example, one could comment on the abortion debate by saying that pro-choice advocates place the emphasis on the Agent and view the fetus in Scenic terms, as natural matter. The Act of abortion, using suction technology as an Agency is morally appropriate in a particular circumstance given the Purposes of the woman, her plans for the future unfolding of her life. Pro-life advocates, on the other hand, think that it is wrong to view the unborn child (note the change in labeling) as mere matter; rather, the unborn child should be treated as an Agent-in-formation (with "rights"). Alternatively, God should be seen as the Agent who is creating the child and abortion is destroying God's work. In either case, the Agent-Scene ratio is interpreted differently than it is by pro-choice advocates, who use the language of individual autonomy to place more emphasis on the woman as Agent. It follows from the pro-life assumptions that the use of abortive technology as an Agency is deemed morally wrong because the Purposes for which it is being employed are not appropriate from the pro-life point of view. A woman should be open to adjusting her life to receive a child (or giving up the child for adoption) instead of controlling her future through an

Act that is viewed as unjust violence.[1] Burke's term "circumference" can also be useful here. Pro-choice advocates commonly speak about the circumstances of a particular woman's life—her financial resources, her relationships or lack thereof, her employment situation, her health, etc. Pro-life advocates commonly talk about abortion in connection with slavery and the Holocaust, by claiming that the fetus is "owned" by the woman as a slave-owner owned slaves, and that the fetus is dehumanized in pro-choice rhetoric just as Hitler dehumanized the Jews.[2] This sort of accusatory rhetoric sounds bizarre and offensive to pro-choice ears. Looked at from Burke's point of view, the difference in perspectives arise out of two disparate circumferences: a focus on the particular situation of a woman vs. placing abortion within the broad Scene of modern history (which is interpreted in a particular way). As Burke says: "the choice of circumference for the scene in terms of which a given act is to be located will have a corresponding effect upon the interpretation of the act itself."[3]

A similar pentadic analysis could be conducted on any controversial issue, such as capital punishment, same-sex marriage, national health-care policy, etc. The question that obviously presents itself is this: Is Burke's pentad simply a tool of description, or can it make a normative contribution to moral thinking? Could a Burke scholar just as easily have pro-choice views as pro-life views because the pentad and Burke's thought more generally has no ethical content or direction? Or does his thought have a direction, a *telos*, that does offer some sort of normativity? This is the question that I am wrestling with, and I have not found any easy answer to it. The fact that there is no easy answer, however, does not logically entail that Burke's thought is purely descriptive.

As a further illustration of the difficulty involved in this question, is it noteworthy that the *KB Journal* web site has published essays with titles such as: "The Question of Kenneth Burke's Ethics," (Timothy Crusius), "Something Completely Different: Notes Toward a Burkean Ethics," (Paul Lynch), and "The Gordian Not: Untangling the Motivorum," (Richard Thames). This latter essay includes an appendix entitled "Essays Towards an Ethics of Motives," which discusses the idea that Burke had in mind not just three main perspectives (grammar, rhetoric, and symbolic), but four, with

---

[1] For another discussion of the pentad and abortion, see Stan A. Lindsay, *Implicit Rhetoric: Kenneth Burke's Extension of Aristotle's Concept of Entelechy* (New York: University Press of America, 1998) 111–28.

[2] See, for example, James Burtchaell, *Rachel Weeping and Other Essays on Abortion* (New York: Andrews and McMeel, 1982) 141–287.

[3] Burke, *A Grammar of Motives*, 77.

the last being an Ethics of Motives. The use of "towards" in this context, and in the title of his early novel, *Towards a Better Life*, suggests that Burke was always reaching in the direction of being able to speak about ethics, but that he felt that in order to do so he needed to clarify another area of thought first.

Alasdair MacIntyre's book *After Virtue* is well known for painting a picture of the modern world as a scene of interminable moral disagreements that arise out the fact that different people begin with different presuppositions. He laments the fact that we are often unaware of our presuppositions, and even if we are aware of them, we seem to have very little skill in having productive arguments about them with others. I view Burke's thought as arising out of a similar intuition about the modern world. It is usually not productive for people to argue about ethics by simply arguing about ethics, because that clash of conclusions does not help us to understand our presuppositions. What comes to light here is the notion that ethics, as a mode of thought, is not sufficient unto itself. Another mode of thought is needed, which can be called anthropological reflection. Ethics is thinking about what human beings ought to do and say (or avoid doing and saying); anthropology is about human beings understanding themselves. What makes us tick? What is going on with us psychologically, sociologically, historically, religiously, etc.? *Understanding* is different from ethically *prescribing*. In my view, Burke grasped this essential distinction, and decided to devote himself to understanding; hence, his emphasis on comprehending human *motives*. He certainly had ethical beliefs and purposes, such as ameliorating the plight of workers oppressed by capitalism, but he intuited that the most effective way for him to make an ethical contribution "towards a better life" was to improve the ability of human beings to reflect on and comprehend the complex nexus of motives that generate human action.

## B.

What did Burke mean by *motives*? As with many of his key terms, he answers this question in various ways.

"What is involved, when we say what people are doing and why they are doing it? An answer to that question is the subject of this book. The book is concerned with the basic forms of thought which, in accordance with the nature of the world as all men necessarily experience it, are exemplified in the attributing of motives."[4] Note here the emphasis on understand-

[4] Burke, *A Grammar of Motives*, xvii.

ing: what and why. A "grammar of ethical judgments," on the other hand, would likely begin with a definition that spoke of what is involved when we apply praise or blame to human actions.

"Thus, if we quizzically scrutinize the expression, 'the motivating of an act,' we note that it implicitly contains the paradox of substance. Grammatically, if a construction is active, it is not passive; and if it is passive, it is not active. But to consider an *act* in terms of its *grounds* is to consider it in terms of what it is not, namely, in terms of motives that, in acting upon the active, would make it a passive."[5] So the meaning of the word motive is inherently paradoxical, in that it implies both a presence and an absence of something external that is moving something internal.

"All gods are 'substances,' and as such are names for motives or combinations of motives."[6] "'Substance' and 'motivation' are convertible terms."[7] So a substance is a motive, but the substance is a paradox, as we just noted.

A "fully-rounded vocabulary of motives will locate motives under all five aspects of our pentad."[8] So scene is a motive, agent is a motive, act is a motive, agency is a motive, and purpose is a motive.

"Order, the Secret, and the Kill. To study the nature of rhetoric, the relation between rhetoric and dialectic, and the application of both to human relations in general, is to circulate about these three motives."[9] By order, Burke means hierarchy, in its myriad manifestations; by secret, he means the interiority of the human person, who is deciding to act; by the kill, he means scapegoating and sacrifice. These three dimensions (which are motives) correspond with Burke's overall concept of grammar, symbolic, and rhetoric. Grammar concerns the vertical axis, the Great Chain of Being, that all beings inhabit in common; the symbolic concerns individual selfhood, the uniqueness of the person's experience of reality (which leads to art); rhetoric concerns the horizontal plane of social relations.[10]

My purpose in marshalling these quotations on "motives" is to demonstrate that Burke's central concern was understanding human behavior, ra-

[5] Burke, *A Grammar of Motives*, 40.
[6] Burke, *A Grammar of Motives*, 43.
[7] Burke, *A Grammar of Motives*, 376.
[8] Burke, *A Grammar of Motives*, 65.
[9] Burke, *A Grammar of Motives and a Rhetoric of Motives*, 789.
[10] Burke, *A Grammar of Motives and a Rhetoric of Motives*, xx, 546–47.

ther than judging it. Even the passages on scapegoating read more like social scientific analysis, than like moralistic denunciations of "evil."[11]

C.

My central thesis, that Burke was hesitant to write as an ethicist because he viewed anthropology as more fundamental (or at least more needed in our time), is supported by the observation that he began *Language As Symbolic Action* with his key "summarizing essay": "Definition of Man." There is no summarizing essay with a title such as "How the Pentad Gives Us Normative Ethics." However, in my analysis of the "Definition" for the next several paragraphs, I will be open to the idea that this essay is a mixture of ethics and anthropology.

Burke's "Definition of the Human" (as I prefer to call it), goes like this:

> Man is the symbol-using (symbol-making, symbol-misusing) animal, inventor of the negative (or moralized by the negative), separated from his natural condition by instruments of his own making, goaded by the spirit of hierarchy (or moved by the sense of order), and rotten with perfection.[12]

Burke chose the word "definition" fully aware of its ambiguity and slipperiness, which he had discussed in "Antinomies of Definition."[13] A "definition," as Burke uses the term here, is a statement that is lyrical, personal, and rhetorical/persuasive, not objective and "scientific." Burke is subtly performing a symbolic act in his activity of defining humans as symbol-users, thus demonstrating his point.

Burke believes that symbolic language is distinctive to humans. Other animals may communicate with grunts, whistles, dances, etc., but human use of symbolic language to create taxonomies, empires, religions, atom bombs, etc., has no analogy among the other animals. Burke believes this point is obvious and irrefutable, though in the wake of Darwin some scientists try to refute it by establishing (or presupposing) continuity between humans and all other creatures. Burke is not "glorifying" our species, simply describing it, when he says: "...birds are spared our many susceptibilities to the ways of

[11] The fact that anthropologist Ernest Becker would see Burke's work as completely compatible with his own attempts at scientific understanding of human behavior is telling in this regard. See Becker, *Escape from Evil*, 144–45.

[12] Kenneth Burke, *Language as Symbolic Action: Essays on Life, Literature, and Method* (Berkeley: University of California Press, 1966) 16.

[13] Burke, *A Grammar of Motives*, 21–38.

demagogic spellbinders. They cannot be filled with fantastic hatreds for alien populations they know about mainly by mere hearsay."[14] This brings to mind two quotations: "...neither lions nor dragons have ever waged such wars with their own kind as men have fought with one another" (St. Augustine), and "...man is the only wild animal" (G.K. Chesterton).[15] Burke's thought is in tune with these quotations, in that he views humanity as being like a runaway train, with no one at the controls. He is wondering how we can gain some control over our symbol-driven motives, given that the symbols seem to be driving us. "An 'ideology' is like a god coming down to earth, where it will inhabit a place pervaded by its presence. An 'ideology' is like a spirit taking up its abode in a body: it makes that body hop around in certain ways; and that same body would have hopped around in different ways had a different ideology happened to inhabit it."[16] Burke's definition says humans are "symbol-making, -using, and -misusing," but in light of what has just been said this seems to be a flaw in the wording of the clause, in that humans are being viewed in the clause as agents rather than recognizing that most of the time in human culture it is symbol-systems (ideologies) that are the real agents that are making us "hop around." Burke is implying that the alleged "autonomy" and self-directedness of the modern individual may be an illusion.

Burke was inspired by reading Henri Bergson to say that the "negative" (thou shalt not) is only present in humans, not in the other animals. Parents say to their young children: "Don't jump on the bed!" "Don't run in the street!" "Don't waste food!" etc. Human socialization is the process of internalizing these negatives so that you say them to yourself. Burke summarizes this point:

> *Action* involves *character*, which involves *choice*; and the *form* of choice attains its perfection in the distinction between Yes and No (between thou shalt and thou shalt not). Though the concept of sheer *motion* is non-ethical, *action* implies the ethical (the human personality). Hence the ob-

---

[14] Burke, *Language as Symbolic Action*, 4–5. Timothy Crusius comments: "...we sometimes 'explain' human brutality as a legacy of the animal's struggle to survive, whereas most of it derives from economic, national, racial, and ethnic ambitions, from social or symbol-driven motives."Crusius, *Kenneth Burke and the Conversation After Philosophy* (Carbondale: Southern Illinois University Press, 1999) 156.

[15] St. Augustine, *City of God*, 12.23; G. K. Chesterton, *Orthodoxy* (Garden City: Doubleday, 1959) 144.

[16] Burke, *Language as Symbolic Action*, 6.

> vious close relation between the ethical and the negatives of the Decalogue.[17]

So we have here a cluster of terms (the negative, action, character, choice, the ethical, human personality) in which "each term implies all the others."[18] For Burke, human beings are distinct from the other animals not only in our symbol using but also in that we are *moral* beings in a way that cannot be affirmed of the other animals. When a hawk kills a squirrel it is not doing something immoral; it is not transgressing a negative; it is simply acting out of a positive instinct. But if a teenage boy were to take a gun and start shooting squirrels for the sheer pleasure of killing, he would be acting *immorally* according to human social standards.

Burke's two ways of formulating this clause (inventor of the negative, or moralized by the negative) play with the same (active/passive) ambiguity we noted in the first clause. To describe humans as inventors seems to imply agency; but no human being now living can claim to be the inventor of the Decalogue and the Negative. We are moralized by, socialized by, the negative, would seem to be more correct, by emphasizing the notion that children are powerfully shaped by their environment.

Friedrich Nietzsche argued in *On the Genealogy of Morality* that the internalization of the negative (bad conscience, guilty feelings) resulted from the transition that humans went through in ancient history from being hunters to being "civilized:"

> Those terrible bulwarks with which state organizations protected themselves against the old instincts of freedom—punishments are a primary instance of this kind of bulwark—had the result that all those instincts of the wild, freed, roving man were turned backwards, *against man himself.* Animosity, cruelty, the pleasure of pursuing, raiding, changing and destroying—all this was pitted against the person who had such instincts: *that* is the origin of 'bad conscience'.[19]

Burke, writing in a very different scene (in the wake of nuclear weapons), argued that we must "make haste to develop the controls (the negatives, the thou-shalt-nots) that become necessary, if these great powers are to be kept from getting out of hand."[20] The great powers he refers to are the

---

[17] Burke, *The Rhetoric of Religion: Studies in Logology* (Boston: Beacon Press, 1961) 41.

[18] Crusius, *Kenneth Burke and the Conversation After Philosophy*, 157.

[19] Friedrich Nietzsche, *On the Genealogy of Morality* (New York: Cambridge University Press, 1994) 61.

[20] Burke, *Language as Symbolic Action*, 13.

State and Technology. For Burke, the negative is a good thing; it is how human beings give some semblance of form and order to their lives. The negative has the potential to rein in the amoral and destructive run-away trains (entelechies) of capitalism, imperialism, and technology.

The next clause, regarding separation from nature, reflects this suspicion of technology just mentioned. Burke believed that our usage of symbols and tools abstracts us from our animal roots, allowing us to "transcend" those roots, to rise up. But this upward movement is paradoxically a *fall* if it leads to environmental destruction, the dis-ease and trained incapacities of urban dwellers when they are outside the city, and the fear that we may destroy ourselves with nuclear weapons. Morality may be a uniquely human phenomenon, but that does not mean that humans as moral beings are disconnected from nature. There is a sense, for Burke, in which humans need to remain connected with their animality, their rootedness in nature, to be ethically healthy.

Moving now to the fourth clause in the "Definition of the Human," we note that Burke believes that there will always be hierarchy in human culture. There will always be apprentices and masters due to differences in time of birth. There will always be political leaders who are giving orders to average citizens. There will always be classes, even in allegedly "communist" societies. If someone says "hierarchy should be replaced with equality," Burke would respond "Just how does the hierarchic principle work in this particular scheme of equality?"[21] Burke is not (conservatively) defending any particular hierarchy; he is asserting that the hierarchical principle is inevitable. Burke says this is a "secular analogue" to the religious concept of "original sin;" this is similar to Paul Ricoeur's "fallible man," though Ricoeur is more comfortable seeing himself as a Christian philosopher, while Burke is in an agnostic tradition sometimes using ideas that have religious analogues. This fourth clause of "Definition" is a deep challenge to all utopian schemes. Like a thinker he admired, William James, Burke is a meliorist (using thought to somewhat improve the human condition), not a pessimist, cynic, or utopian.[22]

[21] Burke, *A Grammar of Motives and A Rhetoric of Motives*, 665.

[22] Crusius, *Kenneth Burke and the Conversation After Philosophy*, 169.

Burke's codicil, "rotten with perfection," occurred to him as an afterthought;[23] though the most common meaning of codicil is a clause added to a will that may alter its meaning significantly. This clause seems to continue the previous clause's warning against utopian schemes, by emphasizing that the entelechial drive in human beings leads us to "improve" our efforts to the maximum degree. Nuclear bombs can be "improved" until they are as destructive as possible; societies can be "improved" by identifying the "perfect enemy" race and putting them in death camps. Burke wants us to use various vocabularies and pieties, playing them off against one another as checks and balances, instead of narrowly using one symbolic vocabulary and "perfecting" it toward what turns out to be a dangerous extreme. Timothy Crusius sums up this point: "...if we can become aware of the entelechial compulsion, then we can also to some extent loosen its hold on us."[24]

I have been arguing that Burke's "Definition" is an example of his choice to focus on anthropology rather than ethics, but there is a deep ambiguity in that idea. This ambiguity is seen in that we have been touching on morality many times in our discussion of the "Definition." The "Definition" is not strictly neutral, objective, and "scientific." A neutral description of human beings might say things such as: we are embodied entities who have to breathe oxygen to survive; we learn language and symbols; we live in groups; we are unique as individuals, even though we are shaped to some extent by social forces, etc. One could make this list as short or as long as one likes, but the essential point is that one could describe human beings by using language that does not involve value judgments. But this is precisely *not* what Burke is doing. He uses words that are loaded with value judgments, such as symbol-misusing, moralized by the negative, separated from nature, goaded by the spirit of hierarchy, *rotten*. In other words, this definition is itself a critique of humanity as a "fallen" species; it is a moral critique of moral creatures. Implicit here is the notion that we are not as we should be, with the faint hope that we could somehow move toward becoming what we should be. To say that Burke wrote about anthropology, not ethics, is thus misleading. He was articulating an ethical critique of humanity in the act of writing about anthropology. That is a more satisfactory description of his overall project. But where does this leave us? How can ethical ideas be developed further out of the trajectory of Burke's thought?

---

[23] An earlier draft of the Definition had been published in *The Rhetoric of Religion* (40) without the codicil.

[24] Crusius, *Kenneth Burke and the Conversation After Philosophy*, 172.

As mentioned above, Timothy Crusius and Paul Lynch have addressed this question in articles which were published in *KB Journal.* Crusius argued, in a short article, that Burkeans can develop their own ethical viewpoints by employing three key concepts: 1) a *comic* perspective would seek to redirect human conflict from actual victimage to being able to laugh at our own foibles and the foibles of others, 2) a *critical* perspective that offers a depth psychology analysis of the human tendency to misuse symbols in preparation for war, 3) an *embodied* perspective that always remembers that human beings are *animals*; this can hold us back from ethical systems that are too abstract, and it can help us to think about living within nature in less destructive ways. Lynch's article builds upon Crusius' by arguing that Burke's thought is an example of casuistry (applying general ethical principles to particular situations). The principles could be those articulated by Crusius, or perhaps other principles, but Lynch's point is that Burke did not make definite moral pronouncements because he wanted to allow for a continual adaptation of actions within varying scenes. One cannot make statements from an Olympian height that are true in all cases; one must continually improvise as one goes along. This does not imply relativism or a complete lack of moral principles; it simply means that the type of "casuistic stretching" that may be appropriate in a given circumstance cannot be predicted ahead of time. [25] I find it notable however, that Crusius' article is so short, and Lynch's article, which is longer, still has very little to say that is directly derived from Burke. Constructing a Burkean ethics seems to be a bit like trying to build a second dwelling utilizing nothing but the scraps of lumber left over from the building of the first one. Burke has left us scraps, hints, and phrases that seem to point in the direction of ethics, but that is all there is to work with.

## D.

Burke is known for his great erudition, but there is a significant body of literature that Burke did not engage in a meaningful way, namely, modern religious thought. One does not find Burke entering into conversation with authors such as Rudolph Bultmann, Karl Barth, Paul Tillich, Reinhold and

[25] Timothy Crusius, "The Question of Kenneth Burke's Ethics," *KB Journal* 3/1 (Fall 2006), accessed March 29, 2019, http://www.kbjournal.org/crusius . Paul Lynch, "Something Completely Different: Notes Toward a Burkean Ethics," *KB Journal* 5/1 (Fall 2008), accessed March 29, 2019, http://www.kbjournal.org/paul_lynch . Burke discusses "Casuistic Stretching" in *Attitudes Toward History*, 3rd ed. (Berkeley: University of California Press, 1984) 229–32.

H. Richard Niebuhr, Eric Voegelin, Dietrich Bonhoeffer, and so forth.[26] We could reach a bit further back in time and refer to Kierkegaard, who is treated in a very limited way in *A Rhetoric of Motives*; the full scope and richness of his thought is not addressed by Burke. I have not found any references to Jonathan Edwards. I raise this issue because it is substantive methodologically. If one sees anthropology as "deeper" or "more fundamental" than ethics, as a mode of thought, one could take the next step and ask what underlies various anthropological visions. This deeper level could be called metaphysics or mysticism or religion. What is "deeper" also turns out to be "higher" in the sense that the divine act of creation is the lowest "sub" under all "sub"-stances, while God also transcends the universe.

Here Burke's personal situation seems to be a limiting factor. He did not see himself as a believer who belonged to a community of faith. He was not hostile toward faith, as evidenced by his respectful references to the Bible, Augustine, Aquinas, and so forth, but he did not personally have a desire to write as a person of faith. One surmises that that influenced his choice of reading material. [27]

Speaking in general terms, Burke's thought lies within the Enlightenment tradition that was framed by authors such as David Hume, Immanuel Kant, Karl Marx, and Friedrich Nietzsche. This tradition, which obviously has great variability, does have a central core in the notion that theological ideas are of historical significance only; they are entirely unnecessary in framing the modern intellectual's world view. Hume, in *The Natural History of Religion*, put forward an account of how belief in the gods arose out of primitive human psychology; Kant was emphatic that the idea of God has no intrinsic connection with moral thought because human reason can always judge the reasonableness of alleged divine commands, thus making their source irrelevant; Marx followed Ludwig Feuerbach in believing that religious ideas are oppressive ideologies that stunt human growth; Nietzsche described Jewish and Christian notions of morality as arising out of the slave's hatred of the master. By placing Burke in this line, I do not mean to

---

[26] Burke contributed an essay to the volume *The Concept of Order*, edited by Paul Kuntz. Eric Voegelin also contributed to that volume, which leads one to believe that they must have been aware of each other.

[27] Wayne Booth sought to convince Burke that he was actually a religious thinker, which Burke rejected as a description (or perhaps not). See "Kenneth Burke's Religious Rhetoric: 'God-Terms' and the Ontological Proof," in *Rhetorical Invention and Religious Inquiry: New Perspectives* (New Haven: Yale University Press, 2000) edited by Walter Jost and Wendy Olmsted, 25–46. See also Edward C. Appel, "Kenneth Burke: Coy Theologian," *Journal of Communication & Religion* 16 (1993): 99–110.

suggest that he agreed with everything they wrote, which would of course be impossible due to internal contradictions, but only to say that Burke's intellectual horizon fits within this broad modern trend that sees theological ideas as historical artifacts rather than as structuring principles in one's own thought world. The alternative is to see theological ideas as living realities, even for "secular" people, precisely because they have structured the Western thought world in general, in a way that is inescapable. Eric Voegelin asserts, for example, that the project of generalizing about human beings is something that happens in the wake of the "revelatory insights" of theology.[28] This places Burke's "Definition" in a different light.

However, paralleling this modern strand of thought, which tends to be dominant in the academy, there is another tradition that argues differently, holding that it is a mistake for human beings to think that a theological worldview is either passé or (privatistically) optional. This strand is seen in Jonathan Edwards, J.G. Hamann, Søren Kierkegaard, and Fyodor Dostoevsky. In the twentieth century, one could point to G.K. Chesterton, Eric Voegelin, and Karl Barth as being on the "God is crucial" side of the fence that Burke did not find himself on. How do these two different traditions handle ethical reflection?

The modernistic / secular strand may find that the human barnyard is simply a tangle of ethical assertions coming from various people and enter into the fray with as much persuasive ability as one can muster. But, the more reflective approach will maintain that when one notices the fray one can then step back from it and seek to think more carefully about human motivations. One can engage in anthropological contemplation, in the hope that doing so will clarify to a certain extent what is happening in human society. If one can persuade others through writing and speaking to see the human condition in a somewhat similar way as oneself, then one can begin to enter into the ethical sphere again with a bit more light and less heat. This seems to me to be Burke's dialectical approach. From ethics to anthropology and then back to ethics (though he never did say very much about ethics that was directly normative).

[28] "Every new insight begins with a single person, who receives it, one might say, as a representative of the whole of humanity. As a matter of fact, the very idea that there is a humanity, that there is a mankind, and that one can generalize about man, appears only when certain revelatory insights occur. These are spiritual outbursts. We now recognize that man is that being who is capable of insight into true order, the order of true existence and of God." Eric Voegelin, "Configurations of History," in *The Concept of Order*, ed. Paul Grimley Kuntz (Seattle: University of Washington Press, 1968) 39.

In the theological strand, however, there is a different method. One can notice the ethical fray, and seek deeper anthropological understanding, but the basic presupposition will be that there needs to be an "upward" turn of attention. People should orient themselves vertically to receive instruction, or commandments, or inspiration, from God, who is the source of all that is. This method is clearly seen in Jonathan Edwards' *The Nature of True Virtue* and in Søren Kierkegaard's *Works of Love*. Here is a sampling of the way Edwards speaks:

> ...those *schemes* of religion or moral philosophy, which—however well in some respects they may treat of benevolence to *mankind*, and other virtues depending on it, yet—have not a supreme regard to God, and love to him, laid as the *foundation*, and all other virtues handled in a *connection* with this, and in *subordination* to it, are not true schemes of philosophy, but are fundamentally and essentially defective.[29]

Edwards was very consciously criticizing David Hume, and similar thinkers, who were forging what became known as the Enlightenment by leaving behind theological modes of thought.[30] Edwards' central argument is that God is the source of all that is and God's character is expressed as benevolence and love toward all that is; true virtue, in human beings, can thus be nothing other than attunement with God through participating in God's "benevolence to being in general." Edwards argues that human beings tend to think that they are being virtuous when they show gratitude to those who have helped them, or when they love friends, relatives, or fellow citizens. However:

> The reason why men are so ready to take these private affections for true virtue, is the narrowness of their views; and above all, that they are so ready to leave the Divine Being out of their view, and to neglect him in their consideration, or to regard him in their thoughts, as though he did not properly belong to the system of real existence, but was a kind of shadowy, imaginary being.[31]

---

[29] Jonathan Edwards, *The Nature of True Virtue* (Eugene: Wipf & Stock, 2003) 26.

[30] George Marsden: "Edwards wrote to John Erskine that he had read Lord Kames' *Essay on the Principles of Morality* (1751) 'and also that book of Mr. David Hume's which you speak of [*A Treatise of Human Nature*]. I am glad of an opportunity to read such corrupt books; especially when written by men of considerable genius; that I may have an idea of the notions that prevail in our nation.'" "Challenging the Presumptions of the Age," in *The Legacy of Jonathan Edwards*, ed. D.G. Hart, Sean Michael Lucas, and Stephen J. Nichols (Grand Rapids: Baker Academic, 2003) 108.

[31] Edwards, *The Nature of True Virtue*, 87.

Note that when Edwards criticizes what he sees as faulty views of virtue, he uses language that directly parallels Burke's comments on having a constricted circumference.[32] That this constriction is morally charged, rather than neutral, is emphasized in this passage:

> Yea, we are apt, through the narrowness of our views, in judging of the beauty of affections and actions, to *limit* our consideration to only a small part of the created system. When private affections extend themselves to a considerable number, we are ready to look upon them as truly virtuous, and accordingly to applaud them highly. Thus it is with respect to a man's love to a large party, or a country. For though his private system contains but a *small part* even of the world of mankind, yet, being a considerable number, they—through the contracted limits of his mind, and the narrowness of his views—are ready to engross his sight, and to seem as if they were *all*. Hence, among the *Romans*, love to their country was the highest virtue; though this affection of theirs, so much extolled, was employed as it were for the destruction of the rest of mankind.[33]

The prescience of this passage, penned by someone known as "America's theologian," is chilling in an age of American imperialism.

Turning now to Kierkegaard, one finds a similar message. In *Works of Love*, Kierkegaard devotes three major chapters to commenting on the meaning of seven words: "you shall love your neighbor as yourself." He says:

> Ultimately, love for God is the decisive factor; from this originates love for the neighbor—but paganism had no inkling of this. It left out God, made erotic love and friendship into love, and abhorred self-love. But the Christian love commandment commands loving God above all else, and then loving the neighbor. In erotic love and friendship, preferential love is the middle term; in love for the neighbor, God is the middle term. Love God above all else; then you also love the neighbor and in the neighbor every human being. Only by loving God above all else can one love the neighbor in the other human being.[34]

When human beings constrict the circumference of their concern, the result is predictable:

> Everyone who in despair has clung to one or another of the dissimilarities of earthly life so that he centers his life in it, not in God, also demands that everyone who belongs to the same dissimilarity must hold together with him—not in the good but in an ungodly alliance against the universally human. The one in despair calls it treason to want to have fellow-

[32] Burke, *A Grammar of Motives*, 77.

[33] Edwards, *The Nature of True Virtue*, 88.

[34] Kierkegaard, *Works of Love*, 57-58.

> ship with others, with all people....Whoever then will love the neighbor, whoever thus does not concern himself with removing this or that dissimilarity, or with eliminating all of them in a worldly way, but devoutly concerns himself with permeating his dissimilarity with the sanctifying thought of Christian equality—that person easily becomes like one who does not fit into earthly life here, not even with so-called Christendom; he is easily exposed to attacks from all sides; he easily becomes like a lost sheep among ravenous wolves. Everywhere he looks, he naturally sees the dissimilarities, and those who in a worldly way have clung firmly to a temporal dissimilarity, whatever it may be, are like ravenous wolves.[35]

What we can see here is not just ethical exhortation, but also what I have been calling in this essay anthropological reflection, built upon theological presuppositions. Kierkegaard is saying, approximately 100 years before the Nazis, that when human beings do not participate in the love of God for all people, then there will be empirically observable aspects of their behavior that flow out of that lack of participation.

This diversion of my argument, into a consideration of Edwards and Kierkegaard, has the purpose of showing that there is an alternative to the narrowed horizon of thought that became popular among European intellectuals in the eighteenth and nineteenth centuries. The essential ambiguity of Burke's thought is that there is a sense in which he is trying to live in both horizons simultaneously. He saw himself as employing "secular analogues" to religious ideas, but in doing so he remained within a *religious* frame. This can be illustrated with reference to Burke's central structuring terms: grammar, symbolic, and rhetoric.

> [O]ur *Grammar of Motives* was constructed about 'substance' as key term, the related rhetoric [focuses on] persuasion and dissuasion, communication and polemic. And our third volume, *Symbolic of Motives*, should be built about *identity* as titular or ancestral term...the thing's *identity* would here be its uniqueness as an entity in itself and by itself. The *Grammar* dealt with the universal paradoxes of substance...The *Symbolic* should deal with unique individuals...The *Rhetoric* deals with the possibilities of classification in its *partisan* aspects; it considers the ways in which individuals are at odds with one another, or become identified with groups more or less at odds with one another...The *Grammar* was at peace insofar as it contemplated the paradoxes common to all men....The *Symbolic* should be at peace, in that the individual substances, or entities, or constituted acts are there considered in their uniqueness, hence outside the realm of conflict. For individual universes, as such, do not compete....But insofar as the individual is involved in conflict with

[35] Kierkegaard, *Works of Love*, 73.

> other individuals or groups, the study of this same individual would fall under the head of *Rhetoric*....The *Rhetoric* must lead us through the Scramble, the Wrangle of the Market Place...Logomachy...War... Rhetoric is concerned with the state of Babel after the Fall."[36]

One way of trying to make sense of this might go like this. There are three main dimensions of reality as it is inhabited by human beings: the vertical axis (the Great Chain of Being), the horizontal plane of social relationships, and the journey through time of the individual person. Another way of expressing this is to say that there are ways we are like everyone else, ways we are like some people and unlike others, and ways we are unique as individuals. We are like everyone in needing to breathe oxygen to survive, like some people in terms of gender, language, nationality, etc., and unique in that we have our own interiority (our thoughts, memories, will). This is a chart I've created to visually represent this:

[36] Burke, *A Grammar of Motives and A Rhetoric of Motives*, 545–46.

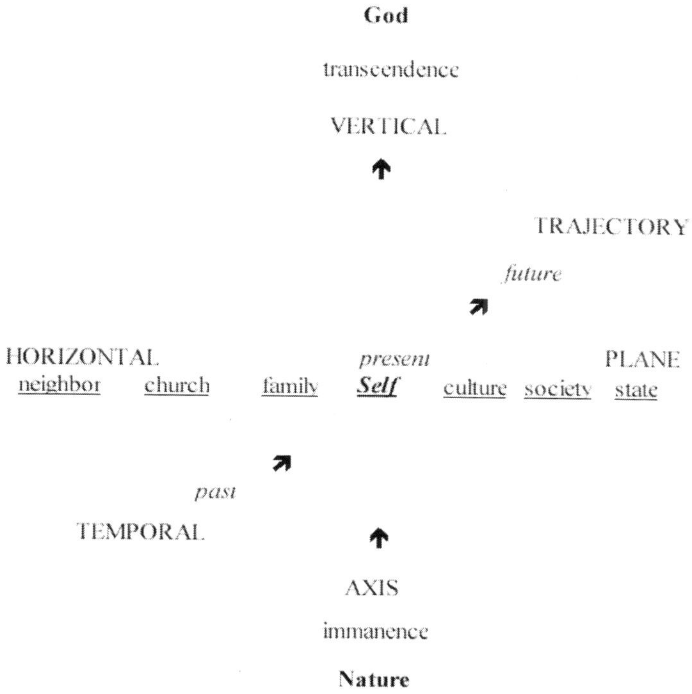


With this as a general scheme, we can say that Burke's *Grammar* has to do mainly with understanding the vertical axis. (The discussion of Substance fits here; Substance is that which lies under, the ground, the physical basis of human life.) The *Rhetoric* will focus on the horizontal plane of community maintenance. The *Symbolic* concerns the individual's experience of reality.

This is a reasonable interpretation of what Burke means to say with his key terms: grammar, symbolic, and rhetoric. But looked at from a theological point of view, what has just been described is the cosmos as the creation of a Triune God. The vertical axis correlates with the work of God the Creator; the trajectory in time of the human self correlates with the Son, the "second Adam"; and the horizontal plane correlates with the Holy Spirit, who is described in the theological tradition as the "bond of love" between the Father and the Son, whose mission is to transform the human community into the kingdom of God. It thus appears to be the case that Burke was using theological concepts without realizing it. Or, if he did realize that that is what he was doing, and he did not say so, then he was guilty of a kind of plagiarism. This issue of philosophical plagiarism bedevils modern secular thought in general, in that ethical values are often affirmed (such as concern for the poor and for victims of injustice, conflict resolution as preferable to war, gender equality, and so forth), which have clearly traceable roots in the Judeo-Christian tradition.[37] There is a kind of "moral yeast" which was introduced into western culture by certain key verses in the Bible, which over the course of many centuries undermined many forms of unethical behavior, such as slavery, burning "heretics" and "witches" at the stake, and so forth.[38] When modern thinkers affirm values such as equality, tolerance, and compassion without realizing that these are the fruits of religious ideals, then there is a lack of historical understanding. There is also a lack of an awareness that such values are historically contingent and fragile phenomena, which may fade away and be replaced with harsher values if the religious communities that incubated that yeast over many centuries cease to exist.

A related lack of understanding is seen when a simplistic equation is drawn which identifies "religion" as the source of violent fanaticism and the "secular" state as the greatest force for peace.[39] The historical record since Hume's time has unfortunately revealed that the most efficient killing machine in the history of the world is the so-called "secular" modern state. In the words of David Hart, "The old order could generally reckon its victims only in the thousands. But in the new age, the secular state, with all its hitherto unimagined capacities, could pursue its purely earthly ideals and ambitions only if it enjoyed the liberty to kill by the millions. How else could it spread its wings?"[40] When human beings decide that they can legitimately invent their own values and enact them politically, the result is rather predictably a rejection of the Chief Negative "Thou shalt not kill." In light of this situation, is it truly prudent to follow the secularist path of thought? It would seem that a very strong case could be made for "modern" people to ask whether or not Edwards and Kierkegaard may have been seeing reality in the light of a divine Sun the eclipse of which has been our downfall. (If one

---

[37] This idea is developed by René Girard, *I See Satan Fall Like Lightning* (Maryknoll, N.Y.: Orbis, 2001) David Hart, *Atheist Delusions: The Christian Revolution and Its Fashionable Enemies* (New Haven: Yale University Press, 2009) and Bruce Ward, *Redeeming the Enlightenment: Christianity and Liberal Virtues* (Grand Rapids: Eerdmans, 2010).

[38] I take the phrase "moral yeast" from Servais Pinckaers, *The Sources of Christian Ethics* (Washington, D.C.: Catholic University of America Press, 1995) 129.

[39] See William Cavanaugh, *The Myth of Religious Violence: Secular Ideology and the Roots of Modern Conflict* (New York: Oxford University Press, 2009).

[40] Hart, *Atheist Delusions*, 223.

were to read that as 'divine Son' the meaning would be basically the same.)

E.

To return to the concept of the dimensions of reality, as a way of wrapping up this essay, we can note that each dimension can become pathological when it is overemphasized and not held in an appropriate balance with the other dimensions. The vertical axis becomes a hierarchical psychosis, for example, when it is used to shape symbolism about the white race being "superior to" the black race, or when terrorists claim to be killing on behalf of God.[41] Selfhood becomes pathological when it is expressed as "the individual *against* the group"; for Burke, excessive individualism is a "fall" that is usually unnoticed. [42] The horizontal plane becomes pathological when a group coalesces for the purpose of victimizing the Other (Nazism, Rwanda, etc.). When we see that the dimensions are *temptations* in the sense that they can become constricted circumferences, then an ethical idea opens up. If the dimensions are narrow limbs that people climb out on in an attempt to avoid living in the Center, in the tensive balance of reality, then an ethical imperative naturally presents itself to us: We *ought*, as human beings, to live within the dimensions in an open, rich, and complex way. Kenneth Burke *was* an ethical thinker in that he intuited the anthropological vision at work here, and he was always reaching towards the elusive goal of complex existence. He saw, as if from a hazy distance, the dimensions, which he labeled grammar, symbolic, and rhetoric, and he saw even further away that this vision presents the ethical imperative to us. The motivorum would be completed by *An Ethics of Motives*.[43]

If we see Burke as always trying to champion the *freedom* of the human spirit in a reductionistic age, and if we see this ethical imperative, living in the Center, as another way of describing the paradox of substance, then we can echo Burke's own language (about substance and motive) by saying that: *living in the Center* and *freedom* are convertible terms.

---

[41] On the latter, see Ruth Stein's analysis of the "vertical" psychosis of the 9/11 hijackers in *For Love of the Father: A Psychoanalytic Study of Religious Terrorism* (Stanford: Stanford University Press, 2010).

[42] Burke, *A Grammar of Motives*, 364.

[43] See Richard H. Thames, "The Gordian Not: Untangling the Motivorum," *KB Journal* 3, no. 2 (Spring 2007), accessed March 29, 2019, http://www.kbjournal.org/thames1 .

# 7

# The Joker Is Satan, and So Are We: Girard and *The Dark Knight*

*The Dark Knight* is a movie that broke box office records. Why? Because it is a powerful expression of theological ideas. I need to elaborate a bit on this apparently odd statement. Let's list, in no particular order, some of the main themes of the movie: The Joker's main goal is not acquiring money, but sowing chaos and destruction; Bruce Wayne and Harvey Dent are rivals for the affection of Rachel Dawes; the police force is filled with corruption; Batman's exploits have produced copycats, imitators; the "law-abiding citizens" and the "criminals" are distinct groups of people…aren't they?...or are they all in the same boat?; a symbol of "justice," such as Harvey Dent, can be seduced to join "the dark side"; criminals often kill each other, taking greed to an irrational extreme. These themes can be elucidated very effectively with reference to the writings of René Girard. [1]

Girard's theory of violence comes to a head in his discussion of Satan. He says that Satan is not a individual person but rather the entire complex event of scapegoating violence. Satan is the seducer who alienates people from God and insinuates to them that they must long for something that they supposedly lack. They must seek out models of success and imitate them. Satan is also the one who "kicks it up a notch" into rivalry, conflict, and chaotic violence. And Satan is the whisperer behind the lynch mob, the voice demanding that One must be sacrificed for the Many. In this way, "law and order" will be restored.

Some scholars have commented, regarding John Milton's poem *Paradise Lost*, that Satan is the most interesting character, much more so than Adam, Eve, the angels, or Christ. In a similar way, the Joker is clearly the most interesting character in *The Dark Knight*, and he is obviously a figura-

---

[1] Author's note: The summary of Girard's mimetic theory in the original article is omitted here to avoid repetition of earlier parts of this book. Charles K. Bellinger, "The Joker Is Satan, and So Are We: Girard and The Dark Knight," *Journal of Religion & Film* 13, Iss. 1, Article 5, accessed March 30, 2019, https://digitalcommons. unomaha.edu/jrf/vol13/iss1/5 .

tive version of Satan. His main purpose is to sow chaos, confusion, and destruction among human beings. He does this by stoking the flames of the *skandalon*—the intense fascination that human beings have with each other in the pursuit of their desires. There is the obvious romantic triangle of Bruce Wayne, Harvey Dent, and Rachel Dawes; two men seeking the affection of one woman is one of the most common mimetic plots. The Joker says to Batman at one point: "Does Harvey know about you and his little bunny?" which throws Batman into a predictable jealous rage. On a larger scale, there is the rivalry between the criminals and the "law abiding citizens," who are all seeking money, mammon. In modern Western culture, which is highly secularized, money is the new god that people worship. The movie is saying that all people are greedy; the difference between the citizens and the criminals is that the latter take greed to an absurd extreme, killing each other off in the process. The Joker recognizes all of this and uses the fascination with money to create all kinds of temptations and conflicts, so that the police become just as corrupt as the criminals.

*The Dark Knight* is a movie that has so many resonances with Girard's ideas that the question inevitably rises as to whether or not the film makers have read him. It may be that his ideas have filtered into the consciousness of the Hollywood intelligentsia. It may be that the comic book authors and the film makers are simply drawing on the same inspirations that Girard draws on: the Bible and great works of literature. The answer to this question is not germane to our discussion here, but it is an interesting sidebar. The quotations from the Joker that I will present shortly have such strong Girardian resonances that it is hard to believe that the film makers have not read Girard. One can speculate that they knew Girard's ideas would make the movie philosophically powerful in addition to being visually dazzling. The combination would be a box office hit because of the public's mimetic desire (word of mouth patronage). The film makers, motivated by a desire to make millions of dollars, employ Girard's ideas. Delicious irony, isn't it?

The interrogation room scene in the middle of movie is its center, where the entire story is revealed under the blinding lights. This scene shows that The Joker is the most astute observer of human pyschology in the film. His insights into mimetic desire and the scapegoating activities of the "civilized" people reveal a transcendent perspective; precisely the sort of transcendent perspective that Girard claims is the fruit of biblical revelation. The Joker says to Batman: "They need you right now. When they don't, they'll cast you out like a leper. You see, their *code*, their *morals*, it's a bad joke." Girard's theory maintains that an individual who is lifted up as a hero today is likely to become the scapegoat tomorrow. The King who is obeyed by his loyal subjects today will have his head chopped off tomorrow. Society sees itself as *moral*, as being comprised of the good people who can judge the bad people. But what society cannot admit to itself is that its need for scapegoats is itself immoral. Society cannot recognize its hypocrisy. The Joker says that "When the chips are down, these *civilized* people, they'll eat each other." He also says "I'm not a monster, I'm just ahead of the curve." He reveals that "law abiding society" is a mystification; human culture is a lynch mob riding the bucking bronco of chaotic violence. By thinking that it is attacking Satan in the form of the scapegoat, society is actually acting according to the satanic principle. When the Joker says "the only sensible way to live in this world is without rules" he is speaking the voice of chaotic, Dionysian violence. But he also reveals in this scene that the "rules," the laws and prohibitions that society invents to contain violence, are a sham. The police and the legal system think of themselves as stemming from a different spiritual source than the demonic criminals; but in reality they all flow out of the fountain of the complex, shapeshifting satanic event. The violence of the criminals and the brutality of the police, symbolized by Batman slamming the Joker's head into the table, reveal that the ultimate basis of violence is reciprocity. The enemies who attack each other come to resemble each other more and more until they are indistinguishable. This is recognized implicitly in the film's underlying question: "How can evil be struggled against without allowing evil to overcome the one who is struggling, turning him to the dark side?"

The Joker's statement to Batman— "You complete me" —is profound, perhaps more profound than the film makers realize. Like the phrase from the gospels, "It is finished," it offers the perfect summary of the entire story. The Joker is saying that his role as the chaotic Satan is complemented by Batman's role as the "law and order" Satan, whose good violence is supposedly casting out the other Satan's bad violence. This is why The Joker can say with such confidence "You have nothing to frighten me with, nothing to do with all your strength." He realizes that Batman is actually his ally in the satanic event. The Joker knows about satanic shapeshifting, Batman does not.

It is customary in movies to present the criminals as evil and the cops as good. But the radical implication of Girard's theory is that evil is present in the structure of "law abiding society;" Satan is ultimately not a person but a complex process. Satan is at work in the actions of the criminal, but when the criminal is apprehended, tried, and retributively punished, society is acting as a lynch mob which is also secretly inspired by Satan. When this is seen, the rhetoric of "Justice" becomes empty, or worse than empty, it becomes the evil of hypocrisy. This is why I say that the film makers may have put into The Joker's mouth a line that is more profound than they realize. To understand that Satan is a shapeshifter who can be in the criminal and in a defender of Justice, such as Harvey Dent or Batman, is to deconstruct the (good guys vs. bad guys) genre of the film. In contemporary political parlance, if the bad guys, the *evildoers*, and those who are carrying out the *War on Evildoing* are all fulfilling Satan's agenda without realizing it, then the world is utterly dark. How can such a world ever change? "Who can deliver us from this body of death?" (Rom. 7:24) This is a question that can only have a christological answer, which is articulated in Romans 12:21: "Do not be overcome by evil, but overcome evil with good." But while the Joker is clearly a Satan figure, it is my argument that Batman is at best an ambiguous Christ figure, in that he willingly accepts the role of scapegoat at the end of the movie. His willingness to use violence within the movie works against the notion that he is a genuine Christ figure.

Christ is not a character in the movie, but he is present throughout, in the sense that his defeat of Satan on the cross, through nonviolent love, puts Satan on display, thus making the revelatory insights of the movie possible. This also is an idea which is articulated clearly by Girard. When the Joker says to Batman "I know the truth. There's no going back. You've changed things forever..." his words intimate that he is really addressing another conversation partner, the same one to whom Dostoevsky's Grand Inquisitor was speaking.

# 8

# Kierkegaard's Critique of Individualism

## I. Introduction

Kierkegaard was often criticized in the middle of the twentieth century for being "too individualistic"; toward the latter part of the twentieth century many leading Kierkegaard scholars developed a response to this charge, claiming that it was based on a faulty reading of his works. I seek to make a complete U-turn on the commentaries that level the charge of "individualism" by arguing that, if we want to criticize individualism in contemporary culture, Kierkegaard is one of the strongest resources we can turn to.

There are various forms of individualism in modern thought: political, economic, epistemological, and so forth. Kierkegaard has most commonly been accused of a theological version of individualism, as in Steven Lukes' comment that Kierkegaard is "the most profound and influential exponent of religious individualism."[1] Similar comments have been made by Louis Mackey, Martin Buber, Karl Barth, Alasdair MacIntyre, and many others. When a charge of this sort is leveled against a thinker, it usually arises out of the intuition that life is very complex, and that Kierkegaard's alleged focus on "the single individual before God" is too narrow, failing to grasp the complexity and relationality that are intrinsic to the human condition. I will show, in response to the critics, that Kierkegaard was deeply aware of the complexity of reality (nature, society, self, time, and God), and argue that he presented a normative vision for balancing these dimensions of reality in a constructive way. His emphasis on "becoming oneself before God" was not a constriction, but actually a gateway that opens out onto life lived in the tension of complex relationality. The individualism that is clearly a prominent aspect of modern culture is deeply opposed to and incompatible with Kierkegaard's relational account of selfhood. In making this case I will draw pri-

[1] Quoted in David Kelsey, *Eccentric Existence: A Theological Anthropology* (Louisville: Westminster John Knox Press, 2009) 1: 394. Pages 391-401 in Kelsey provide an overview of various forms of individualism and how they are commonly criticized.

marily on key works in the second authorship, such as *Christian Discourses*, *The Sickness unto Death*, "Purity of Heart," and *Works of Love*.

## II. Kierkegaard's Complex Vision of Selfhood

In Part One of *Christian Discourses*, Kierkegaard paints a picture of life as lived by three different types of agents: the lilies and the birds, the pagan, and the Christian. The lilies and birds, spoken of by Christ in the gospel, are representatives of the realm of nature. They do not worry and fret; they do not concern themselves with poverty or wealth, lowliness or loftiness; they are not presumptuous or suicidal; they do not glance here and there to compare themselves enviously with others. They simply are what they are; they naturally and continually live in accord with God's will. Kierkegaard thus refers to them as God's "assistant teachers" in the art of living.[2] We ought to learn from them what it means to be a creature of God.

The "pagan," described by Kierkegaard in generalized terms, actually sinks down into a miserable state that is lower than the lilies and the birds, because he can fail to be a human being, in contrast to the lilies and the birds who can never fail to be what they are. One fails to be a human being by alienating oneself from God; to truly be a human being *requires* "being before God."[3] In this state of disconnection from the vertical relationship with the Creator, the pagan becomes lost in a morass of horizontal relationships with other human beings:

> From "the others" a person actually finds out only what the others are—it is in this way that the world wants to deceive a person out of becoming himself. "The others" in turn do not know what they themselves are either but continually know only what "the others" are. There is only one who completely knows himself, who in himself knows what he himself is—that is God. And he also knows what each human being is in himself, because he is that only by being before God. The person who is not before God is not himself either, which one can be only by being in the one who is in himself. If one is oneself by being in the one who is in himself, one can be in others or before others, but one cannot be oneself merely by being before others.[4]

[2] Kierkegaard, *Christian Discourses*, 9.

[3] Kierkegaard, *Christian Discourses*, 44.

[4] Kierkegaard, *Christian Discourses*, 40.

Notice the logic of Kierkegaard's argument here. In order to be in real relationships with other human beings, one must be a human being—which is only possible as the fruit of an openness to God. Love of God makes possible love of self and love of neighbor. The pagan, however, because of his rejection of relationship with God, sinks into a state of nothingness, a ghostly lack of selfhood. The "community" that is generated by a conglomeration of such ghosts hardly deserves the name "community" because it is nothing but a horizontal plane within which everyone is looking at everyone else in an endless hall of mirrors. As if Kierkegaard's message was not clear enough already, he drives home his point by referring to the verse: "Let us kill the son, and the vineyard is ours" (Matt. 21:38). The pagan's alienation from God is not just forgetfulness or lack of attention; it is actually an attempt to kill God, or at least to "kill the thought of him."[5] But because to be a human being is only possible through relationship with God, the attempt to "slay God is the most dreadful suicide."[6]

The Christian, in contrast, is, quite simply, a *human being*, just as the bird is a bird. The Christian is different from the bird, however, in that she is conscious that she has been created by God in God's *image* [*Billede*]. She knows, further, that God has come down in the Incarnation and dwelt among us, so that we would have a *prototype* [*Forbillede*] to follow.[7] To be a human being is to be like Christ, because he is the embodiment of what it is to be a human being. The Christian believes that if she seeks to resemble the prototype, she will be brought "into kinship with God," because she will have God not "only as a creator, as all creatures do," but as her "brother."[8] This is a remarkable statement, because it brings the vertical relationship with God down to earth and resituates it on the horizontal plane. The dimensions of reality are being knit together, in an anthropological vision that is a stark contrast to atomistic individualism.

*The Sickness unto Death* begins with the famous paragraphs in which Kierkegaard describes the self as a synthesis of the eternal and the temporal, the infinite and the finite, freedom and necessity. The self is a complex event that happens at the intersection of these dimensions, and the health of the self is found when this synthesis happens in and through relationship with God, the power that creates the self. The sickness of the self occurs when the synthesis is not maintained in a balanced and complex way, and when

[5] Kierkegaard, *Christian Discourses*, 66.
[6] Kierkegaard, *Christian Discourses*, 67.
[7] Kierkegaard, *Christian Discourses*, 41.
[8] Kierkegaard, *Christian Discourses*, 43.

the human being is either thoughtlessly ignorant of God or actually in rebellion against God. Note how for Kierkegaard the ideal of selfhood is not being in one's own little world, cut off from relationship with others; the ideal is relationship with God, and finding one's true selfhood through relationship with Christ, who is the "criterion and goal" of selfhood that we ought to adopt as a model for our thinking and acting.[9]

Sin is understood by Kierkegaard as a refusal to take Christ as a model, which means that one is rejecting the possibility of becoming oneself before God. The effects of sin are described as lacking a self "in a deeper sense"; any other loss, such as "five dollars, or a wife, is sure to be noticed."[10] The human being who lacks a self will want to hide in a crowd, to be just like others, a "mass man." People who live in this way have "no self before God—however self-seeking they are otherwise."[11] Notice that to lack a self does not prevent a person from being selfish and narcissistic. Indeed, the motive driving the refusal to become a self is a longing for self-centered isolation. This is the paradox at the heart of Kierkegaard's anthropology, which is derived from the gospel saying: "For whosoever will save his life shall lose it: and whosoever will lose his life for my sake shall find it" (Matt. 16:25). Individualism, in the negative sense, is preferring one's own selfish small-mindedness to the expansive and complex selfhood-in-relationality into which God is calling all people.

Kierkegaard's discourse on the theme "Purity of Heart Is to Will One Thing" provides guidance for the human soul that is open to this dynamic event of leaving behind the pathway of evasion and entering into the way of spiritual growth. The human being who is hiding from God, and thus from selfhood-in-a-deeper-sense, will seek to hide within a crowd, and the crowd will become a violent mob that will either attack a scapegoat or another crowd. Kierkegaard seeks to disentangle his readers from the crowd and lead them through the gateway of becoming oneself before God, which leads to a new way of relating to other people. Instead of the worldly dynamic that dictates clinging to others who belong to one's in-group and hating those who belong to an enemy out-group, the person who wills one thing in truth

[9] Kierkegaard, *The Sickness unto Death*, 114.
[10] Kierkegaard, *The Sickness unto Death*, 32–33.
[11] Kierkegaard, *The Sickness unto Death*, 35.

and lives in relation to God will exist in "harmony" with other human beings and embrace the "universally human;" he or she will live "in concordance with all people." [12]

For Kierkegaard, to become a "single individual before God" is not an end in itself; it is a movement, a leap, from one way of living to another. I am reminded here of the Wood Between the Worlds in C.S. Lewis' *The Magician's Nephew*. To become an individual, a self-in-the-deeper-sense, is to go through a gateway and come out the other side living in a different world. The fallen, sinful world is characterized by a lack of true selfhood, by a mob mentality, and by evasion of relationship with God. The other world, that we are invited to enter, is characterized by openness to growth in selfhood, by love of neighbor, and by seeing all things in relation to God. Kierkegaard calls this "seeing by means of eternity's light." [13]

The heart of the message conveyed in *Works of Love* is a commentary on the Greatest Commandment: you shall love God, and your neighbor as yourself. This crucial message of Jesus is unpacked by Kierkegaard as a triangulation of three elements: hearing the royal law, the *shall*; loving the neighbor as a *thou* distinct from oneself; and loving oneself in the proper way. Throughout the book these three are contrasted with mutiny against God, a failure to love the neighbor, and the selfishness that lies at the root of preferential, worldly love. Kierkegaard is painting a picture of the complexity of human life in these three dimensions: the vertical relationship with God; the horizontal relationship with other human beings; and the journey of the self through time.

Those who accuse Kierkegaard of excessive individualism can make no sense whatsoever of a passage such as this:

> Love is a need, the deepest need, in the person in whom there is love for the neighbor; he does not need people just to have someone to love, but he needs to love people. Yet there is no pride or haughtiness in this wealth, because God is the middle term, and eternity's *shall* binds and guides this great need so that it does not go astray and turn into pride. But there are no limits to the objects, because the neighbor is all human beings, unconditionally every human being.
>
> Therefore the one who truly loves the neighbor loves also his enemy. The distinction *friend* or *enemy* is a difference in the object of love, but love for the neighbor has the object that is without difference. The neighbor is the utterly unrecognizable dissimilarity between persons or is the eternal equality before God—the enemy, too, has this equality. People think that

[12] Kierkegaard, *Upbuilding Discourses in Various Spirits*, 144.

[13] Kierkegaard, *Works of Love*, 89.

> it is impossible for a human being to love his enemy, because, alas, enemies are hardly able to endure the sight of one another. Well, then, shut your eyes—then the enemy looks just like the neighbor. Shut your eyes and remember the commandment that you shall love; then you love—your enemy—no, then you love the neighbor, because you do not see the dissimilarities of earthly life, but enmity is also one of the dissimilarities of earthly life. Moreover, when you shut your eyes, your mind is not distracted and confused just when you are supposed to listen to the words of the commandment. When your mind is not confused and distracted by looking at the object of your love and the dissimilarity of the object, you become all ears for the words of the commandment, as if it spoke only to you, that *you* shall love the neighbor. See, when your eyes are closed and you have become all ears to the commandment, then you are on the way of perfection to loving the neighbor. [14]

It is clear that this passage is christological; Christ loved his enemies; he embodied this "deepest need," to love the neighbor. But the Christian is supposed to follow this model, not reject it:

> Just as Christianity's joyful message is contained in the doctrine of humanity's inherent kinship with God, so is Christianity's task humanity's likeness to God. But God is love, and therefore we can be like God only in loving, just as we also, according to the words of the apostle, can only be *God's co-workers—in love*. . . . when you love the neighbor, then you are like God. [15]

The so-called "love" that is present in preferential love is actually a form of narcissistic closed-upness. It is only love of neighbor, as described by Kierkegaard, that allows the other human being to actually be an other. The neighbor is the first *thou* (WL, 57). [16] Individualism, in the negative sense, never has a true encounter with another human being as a *thou*.

Kierkegaard paints an either/or picture of human life. We *either* live within the framework of a small-minded selfishness, which has its roots in a lack of relationship with God and produces the poisonous fruit of a mob mentality, *or* we respond to God's call of creation, allowing ourselves to grow into mature selfhood as we journey through time, and loving all other human beings as our neighbors. Small-minded selfishness is individualism, in the negative sense, and that is what Kierkegaard is criticizing; he articulates a positive vision of the person as woven into the fabric of reality. The person

---

[14] Kierkegaard, *Works of Love*, 67–68.

[15] Kierkegaard, *Works of Love*, 62–63.

[16] Kierkegaard, *Works of Love*, 67. I prefer the earlier Hong translation 'first thou' to the later 'first you.'

arises out of nature as a creature of God, she finds her spiritual health through loving forth love in other human beings, and she is in her own personhood a relation that relates itself to itself—in relation to God.

# 9

# The Kierkegaard-Girard Option

Our world has been shaped by the thinking of intellectuals. Usually, the average citizen has bouncing around in his or her mind fragments of thoughts that were articulated by the leading thinkers of two, three, or five hundred years ago. Or, this citizen may have fragments bouncing around that were not exactly articulated as such by the old thinkers, but instead it is the unforeseen ramifications of the ideas of those authors, as they have morphed over time. Brad Gregory's book, *The Unintended Reformation*, [1] for example, argues that certain important aspects of our culture, such as individualism, secularization, and interminable moral arguments can be traced back to Martin Luther, although these developments were not what he intended.

I make this point about the influence of intellectuals to set the stage for this final chapter. All of us, not just the intellectual elites and professors, need to pay more attention to the thoughts in our heads. We need to become more philosophically coherent and competent. We need to be able to engage in more productive conversations with other citizens who have different views than ours. Only in this way can we make real progress toward making the world better.

The format of this chapter is as follows. I will summarize three books on the current scene that I find to be flawed: Mark Juergensmeyer on religion and violence, Jonathan Haidt on moral psychology, and Kate Greasley on abortion; these summaries will be responded to by drawing on other authors I find to be more helpful and truth-speaking. Juergensmeyer will be responded to by Richard Weaver, René Girard, and Eric Voegelin. Haidt will be responded to by Servais Pinckaers, Shelby Steele, and Ms. Daryl Koehn.[2] Greasley will be responded to by Chantal Delsol, Giorgio Agamben, and Søren Kierkegaard. The respondents will focus our attention in

---

[1] Brad Gregory, *The Unintended Reformation: How a Religious Revolution Secularized Society* (Cambridge, Mass.: Harvard University Press, 2012).

[2] I add the "Ms." because the reader may not know whether this author is a man or a woman. Her last name is pronounced "Cain."

helpful ways within the dimensions of historical understanding, horizontal / social awareness, and selfhood.

I will conclude with an overview of what I am proposing as the "Kierkegaard-Girard Option." What are implications of these ideas for such culture wars issues as abortion, same-sex marriage, and the meaning of "conscience protections" in our age? My goal is to give my reader tools for thinking and ideas for conversation, not definitive and exhaustive analyses.

## Topic One: Religion and Violence

### *Mark Juergensmeyer: Cosmic War*

Mark Juergensmeyer's book *Terror in the Mind of God: The Global Rise of Religious Violence* was first published in the year 2000. At that time, he had been studying the topic of religion and violence for many years already, and was a widely recognized expert on the subject. After the 9/11 attacks, he was interviewed on various media outlets, and he has continued to write and lecture widely on this subject up to the present day. He has had a long and distinguished career as a professor of sociology, political science, and religious studies. The book we are considering here is now in its fourth edition (2017) [3] and it is widely assigned as a textbook as well as being read by journalists and members of the general public who want to develop a better understanding of the relationship between religion and violence. Unfortunately, I cannot actually say that it is a good book.

The outline of the book has two main parts: the first provides a survey organized by religious tradition, with chapters on Christianity, Judaism, Islam, Sikhism, and Buddhism; the second seeks to provide a "theoretical" answer to the question of why religious people are so often violent. The strength of the first part would seem to be that it is not just arm-chair scholarship, in that it includes accounts of interviews that the author personally conducted with terrorists or their ideological supporters; but this turns out to be a weakness in the end. I will explain why later. The second part of the book is a collection of essays on "violence as theater," on "struggling against cosmic evil," on "martyrs and demons," and on masculinity. The final chapter, which is supposed to provide sage advice on this vexing problem, has very little to say that it is helpful. It just peters out.

Why is the book such a disappointment? Consider his choice of examples in the "Christianity" chapter: Timothy McVeigh, Anders Breivik (who

---

[3] Mark Juergensmeyer, *Terror in the Mind of God: The Global Rise of Religious Violence*, 4th ed. (Berkeley: University of California Press, 2017).

shot to death teenage members of a liberal political party in Norway), Northern Ireland, and Paul Hill (who shot and killed an abortion doctor). By the author's own admission, McVeigh and Breivik were not church-going individuals, and he has to grasp at straws to loosely connect them to right-wing political groups that have only the remotest and most tenuous connection to anything resembling historic Christianity. The violence in Northern Ireland was always primarily political, and the notion that the "Shankill Butchers" committed acts of torture and murder *because* they were "Protestants" is so obviously ludicrous that Juergensmeyer does not even attempt to make such an argument. The killing of an abortion doctor by an anti-abortion zealot is actually the most cogent example given here of how "Christianity" could motivate a person to kill, because Paul Hill and his mentor Mike Bray did actually think through what Hill was intending to do based on their reading of the Bible and their theological formulations. But these are marginal characters, whose actions have been consistently and resoundingly condemned by all of the mainstream pro-life advocacy groups. Juergensmeyer assumes, correctly of course, that Hill was acting immorally, but the lack of any substantive engagement with moral philosophy throughout the book renders the author unable to explain why. In sum, Juergensmeyer has completely failed to show that "Christianity" as a complex tradition fits within an account of how "religion" as a phenomenon somehow "motivates" human beings to commit acts of violence. The scare quotes are necessary precisely because what Christianity is and what religion is remains opaque and uncomprehended, not just in this chapter, but in the book as a whole.

The section on ISIS raises the same issue noted above regarding Breivik and McVeigh; Juergensmeyer says quite clearly that ISIS is more political than religious, and it is considered as such by most Muslims. The author never clearly explains how "religious" motives could be distinguished from "political" ones. Another structural issue with this book is that the first part is organized according to religions, such as Christianity or Buddhism, even though some of the behaviors Juergensmeyer describes are clearly regional in nature—Northern Ireland, or Myanmar, or the Middle East. Atrocities and acts of revenge for atrocities are sometimes *within* "religions" and sometimes *between* them, which clearly calls for a different interpretive strategy than the one which Juergensmeyer employs. The distinction between lone wolves, and more clearly social phenomena, also needs more clarification than the author gives it.

The second half of the book shifts from describing behaviors to the author's own theoretical framework, which focuses on the notion of "cosmic war"—human beings engage in acts of violence if they believe that they are on the side of light and are struggling against the forces of darkness. This allows people to justify violent acts in their own eyes, even terrible atrocities such as the killing of children. But the author does not ask why some people believe that they are involved in this "cosmic war" while others do not; these others may, in fact, be passionately devoted to religiously motivated peacemaking. Juergensmeyer also does not ask his interviewees probing questions about how they understand the nature of God, and how they connect God with the authorization of violence. His ear is not tuned to listen for such theological talk, which renders his title very problematic. He is not actually writing about terror in the mind of God, but only about terror in the mind of particular disturbed human beings. Nazism and Communism are also outside this book's scope, which indicates that the author is not really serious about understanding violence as a psychological and cultural phenomenon, within which "religion" and "political religions" would be facets.

This book's deficiencies in both theology and anthropology require supplement from deeper thinkers. Juergensmeyer notes, for example, that people who commit violent acts often seem normal, sane, and morally upright, but he does not draw on what Aristotle and Thomas Aquinas say: "All action intends a good"—but not all action *is* good because of faulty reasoning about means and ends. Søren Kierkegaard is also helpful in reflecting on sin and violence as resistance to the divine call to grow in maturity of selfhood, which entails love of God and neighbor. Kenneth Burke brought into articulation very subtle and probing questions about human "motives"—precisely the sort of questions that do not appear on Juergensmeyer's radar screen. René Girard's profound insights into mimetic desire, rivalry, and the scapegoat mechanism are mentioned in passing, but Juergensmeyer seems tone-deaf to the immense significance of Girard's theory, even though he is familiar with it.

I mentioned above that the interviews would seem to be a strength of the book, but they are actually a weakness. Imagine that a psychiatrist goes to a mental hospital and meets a particular patient for the first time. The psychiatrist says: "Give me a clear and complete self-diagnosis; explain to me why you are insane." The scene is ludicrous, of course, but why? An insane person is such precisely because he or she is inarticulate and uncomprehending of his or her situation. Yet this is Juergensmeyer's method. He is asking the morally insane, the violent ones, to explain why they are violent; and he takes them at their word. He works with their words to develop his "theory" about "struggling against cosmic evil." If the insane are actually to be understood, the understanding must come from the outside, from the psychiatrist, who has a level of maturity, intelligence, and stability that the crazy people lack. The difference between Juergensmeyer's book on "religion and violence" and a good one is that the latter will always have the implicit epigraph: "They know not what they do."

*Richard Weaver: The Impious Modern Mind*

Richard Weaver, a professor of English, Rhetoric, and Philosophy at the University of Chicago, published *Ideas Have Consequences* in 1948; it was his attempt to make sense of the debacle of the rise of Nazism and Communism and the vast destruction caused by World War II. He has a very long historical view, reaching back to the late Middle Ages, arguing the rejection of the philosophical realism represented by Thomas Aquinas, in favor of the philosophical nominalism represented by William of Ockham, was the fateful turn in Western intellectual history. "The defeat of logical realism in the great medieval debate was the crucial event in the history of Western culture; from this flowed those acts which issue now in modern decadence."[4] Nominalism has slowly but surely infected the Western mind to such an extent that its presuppositions about reality are now so deeply engrained in us that it is as if we are fish swimming in nominalist waters who are unable to form any mental conception of what life on dry land would look like. Realism is the idea that reality is capable of being understood by the human mind, when human beings adopt an attitude of humility and openness to learning from reality. Reality is the Master and human beings are Apprentices. Nominalism is the notion that reality is beyond the reach of the human mind; therefore our intellectual task can be nothing other than inventing interpretive schemes which we use to make sense of reality and control it. Reality is clay to be molded by the human will and intellect.

Weaver argues that the acceptance of nominalism has led to three main impieties in the modern world: contempt for history, domination of nature, and the mass killing of other human beings in "holocausts and wars." Nazism and Communism were two different examples of the consequences of nominalism; they both saw reality as clay to be molded through the killing of human beings. Those of us in the West who are not Nazis or Communists think that we are innocent, that we are morally righteous. But to the extent that we are fish swimming in nominalist waters we are deceiving ourselves. Our form of nominalism is extreme individualism. Weaver says that the "modern position seems only another manifestation of egotism, which de-

---

[4] Richard Weaver, *Ideas Have Consequences* (Chicago: University of Chicago Press, 1948) 3.

velops when man has reached a point at which he will no longer admit the right to existence of things not of his own contriving. From somewhere in his self-centered being he brings plans which he would truculently impose . . ." in an effort to secure "an unconditional victory over nature." Modern egotism "denies any source of right ordering outside itself. It is belligerence toward the nonself."[5] Our only hope for reassembling our fragmented selves and culture is a renewed "spirit of piety" in three things, "nature, our neighbors—by which I mean all other people—and the past."[6] The root of violence, for Weaver, is not "religion," but rather its opposite, which he describes as the "modern formula" of demanding unconditional surrender from nature and from other human beings; this "impiously puts man in the place of God by usurping unlimited right to dispose of the lives of others." We ought to "have enough imagination to see into other lives and enough piety to realize that their existence is a part of beneficent creation [which] is the very foundation of human community." Instead, we are either barbarians who "destroy what is different because it is different," or we are neurotics, who demand the "control of others, probably because [our] own integration has been lost."[7]

I am only scratching the surface of a profound and important work. I urge my reader to take and read it.

*René Girard: Hypocrisy as the Engine of Culture*

I have already written extensively about René Girard earlier in this book, so I can be very brief here. Juergensmeyer quotes Dr. Abdul Aziz Rantisi, one of the leaders of Hamas: "You think we are the aggressors. . . . That is the number one misunderstanding. We are not: we are the victims."[8] This is how Rantisi justified in his own mind the suicide attacks carried out by Hamas against Israeli civilians. The Israelis, of course, see themselves as victims also, first of the Nazis and then of the Palestinians. Everyone wants to claim the mantel of victimhood, so that the violence they carry out will be justified in their own minds. This is precisely what Girard's thought illuminates with such a powerful spotlight. We live in an age of victim chic, precisely because our world has been so deeply and subtly influenced by the Bible for three thousand years. But we are only semi-converted by the Bible's unveiling of the scapegoat mechanism if we employ the rhetoric of victim-

[5] Weaver, *Ideas Have Consequences*, 171–72.

[6] Weaver, *Ideas Have Consequences*, 172.

[7] Weaver, *Ideas Have Consequences*, 175.

[8] Juergensmeyer, *Terror in the Mind of God*, 4th ed., 92.

hood as a justification for violence. In our semi-converted state we can only unwittingly bear witness to the truth that *hypocrisy is the fallen human condition.* We accuse others of being violent when we ourselves are being violent. To be fully converted would be to abandon the victim chic mentality and truly imagine a world without scapegoating. We need to reimagine how we inhabit the horizontal plane of sociality and stop creating in-groups and out-groups. Yes, that is easier said than done, but it must be done.

*Eric Voegelin: The Consequences of Deicide*

The fateful turn to nominalism that Weaver spoke of was initially carried out within debates between different Christian thinkers in the late Middle Ages, but the outflow of nominalist victory has led to the secularization of modern thought in the natural sciences, the social sciences, and the humanities. Eric Voegelin's life project was to unveil the consequences of this secularization and prophetically stand up against it. Voegelin was one of those many thinkers who had to flee from Nazi Germany in the 1930s, because he had already written books exposing the racism of the Nazi version of political religion. His writings also contain a profound critique of Karl Marx as a phony, a philosophical swindler who prohibited anyone who followed him from asking the most vital questions about morality and human existence.[9] He finds the deeper level commonality between right-wing fascism and left-wing communism in the concept of Gnosticism: "Gnostic man no longer wishes to perceive in admiration the intrinsic order of the cosmos. For him the world has become a prison from which he wants to escape."[10]

At the heart of modernity there is a rejection of the perennial philosophy articulated in Plato, Aristotle, the Bible, Augustine, and Aquinas. This rejection opens up the door for human beings to shape reality according to their immature and diseased wills. The purpose of Marx's speculation "is to shut off the process of being from transcendent being and have man create himself."[11] Genuine philosophy, Voegelin argues, "springs from the love of being; it is man's loving endeavor to perceive the order of being and attune himself to it. Gnosis desires dominion over being; in order to seize control of being the gnostic constructs his system."[12] The deepest motive at work in

---

[9] Eric Voegelin, *Modernity Without Restraint: The Political Religions, The New Science of Politics, and Science, Politics, and Gnosticism* (Columbia: University of Missouri Press, 2000) 264.

[10] Voegelin, *Modernity Without Restraint*, 254–55.

[11] Voegelin, *Modernity Without Restraint*, 262.

[12] Voegelin, *Modernity Without Restraint*, 273.

thinkers such as Marx and Nietzsche, and their progeny, Lenin, Stalin, and Hitler, is "the murder of God." To create a new world, a second reality, after the first reality as it comes from the hand of the Creator has been rejected, "the givenness of the order of being must be obliterated; the order of being must be interpreted, rather, as essentially under man's control. And taking control of being further requires that the transcendent origin of being be obliterated: it requires the decapitation of being—the murder of God."[13] What begins as a speculative formulation of thought becomes action in history, about which thousands of books subsequently need to be written: "Historically, the murder of God is not followed by the superman, but by the murder of man: the deicide of the gnostic theoreticians is followed by the homicide of the revolutionary practitioners."[14]

Voegelin's thought is not only critical; he also articulates a positive and normative vision of a sound philosophical anthropology, describing the "primordial community of being" that is made up of God, the cosmos, persons, and society. Human beings know this community by virtue of their participation "in the mystery of its being."[15] The concept of dimensional anthropology forms the backbone of Voegelin's worldview and positive message. In the passage just referred to, God and the cosmos / world refer to the vertical axis of spirit and matter; society refers to the horizontal plane; and "man" (or the person) refers to the existence of the individual self in time. The ideal for human beings is living within the matrix of these dimensions in a way that is rich, complex, symphonic, balanced. False philosophies, and their outflow in violence, result from the refusal of human beings to maintain this balance.

I am only scratching the surface of Voegelin's immense and erudite corpus of works, which spans thirty-four volumes in its collected edition. Juergensmeyer served a term as the President of the American Academy of Religion; there is no Eric Voegelin section within that academy. These two facts, juxtaposed, reveal the priorities of today's intellectual elites in the study of religion.

---

[13] Voegelin, *Modernity Without Restraint*, 278.

[14] Voegelin, *Science, Politics, and Gnosticism*, 48.

[15] Voegelin, *Order and History: Volume One, Israel and Revelation*, 1.

## Topic Two: Moral Psychology

### *Jonathan Haidt: The Self-Righteous Mind*

We turn next to another widely read book: Jonathan Haidt's *The Righteous Mind: Why Good People Are Divided by Politics and Religion.*[16] The cover features prominently a quote from *The New York Times Book Review*, describing the book as "A landmark contribution to humanity's understanding of itself."

While this is another flawed book, it does at least demonstrate the virtue of clarity of argument in exemplary fashion. The prose is lucid and helpful summaries are provided along the way. Haidt is a social psychologist who has taught at the University of Virginia and New York University.

Haidt's central argument is expressed in his most memorable image: the rider on the elephant. The "elephant" is our emotions and moral intuitions; the "rider" is our reason, which comes along *ex post facto* to provide a rationalization for whatever the elephant has decided to do. With this image, argued and elaborated over multiple chapters, Haidt claims to have shown that Plato was wrong and Hume was right about morality. Plato initiated what Haidt calls "the rationalist delusion," namely that our situation should likened to a rider controlling a well-trained horse; Hume's project, in contrast, made the "philosophically sacrilegious claim that reason was nothing but the servant of the passions." [17] Haidt summarizes his first key argument as: "Intuitions come first, strategic reasoning second."[18] It is interesting to note that this insight places him in the correct frame of mind to avoid the central error made by Juergensmeyer; Haidt does recognize that most human beings, most of the time, are not actually acting in a certain way because of their conscious reasoning; they know not what they do. "The elephant," he says, "is the other 99 percent of our mental processes—the ones that occur outside of awareness but that actually govern most of our behavior."[19]

If the elephant, not "reason," is actually in charge, then we can understand why debates about moral issues are so difficult for "liberals" and "conservatives" to have productive conversations about. To be liberal or conservative, in Haidt's world, is simply to be riding a different sort of elephant, with different intuitions. One aspect of the book is Haidt's honesty regarding

[16] Jonathan Haidt, *The Righteous Mind: Why Good People Are Divided by Politics and Religion* (New York: Vintage Books, 2012). Haidt is pronounced "height."

[17] Haidt, *The Righteous Mind*, 34.

[18] Haidt, *The Righteous Mind*, xx.

[19] Haidt, *The Righteous Mind*, xxi.

how the research for the book opened up his mind to recognize more than just the first three taste receptors, or intuitive senses, that liberals such as himself draw on: (1) harm and suffering,(2) fairness and justice, and (3) liberty. Haidt came to realize in the course of writing that conservatives have those three taste receptors, but also three more that tend to be downplayed by liberals: (4) loyalty, (5) authority, and (6) sanctity. This greater range of sources can often give conservative politicians a leg up when appealing to the intuitions of voters.

Haidt continues his argument by claiming that "morality binds and blinds," a phrase that correlates with "human beings are 90 percent chimp and 10 percent bee."[20] Here his scientism and evolutionary perspective comes through clearly. We are, from one angle, very advanced primates; from another, we are "hive" creatures whose existence in groups blinds us to deeper moral truths and leads to in-group altruism and out-group genocide. He thus concludes his Introduction with this rather striking observation, coming from an agnostic scientist:

> In the coming chapters I'll draw on the latest research in neuroscience, genetics, social psychology, and evolutionary modeling, but the take-home message of the book is ancient. It is the realization that we are all self-righteous hypocrites:
>
> Why do you see the speck in your neighbor's eye, but do not notice the log in your own eye?...You hypocrite, first take the log out of your own eye, and then you will see clearly to take the speck out of your neighbor's eye. (Matthew 7:3–5)

One might think that on the basis of this apparent respect for a key teaching of the New Testament, the author would have shown more curiosity about what the Bible and religious tradition more generally teach about human nature and about morality, but, alas, such is not the case.

The overall atmosphere of the book cannot escape from the limitations of scientism as an approach to thought. The author seems to think that conducting public opinion surveys will somehow give "science" and "evolutionary theory" special insights into moral philosophy. This is an example of the naturalistic fallacy at its worst. One cannot simplistically transition from observations of behaviors to moral evaluations of them. Haidt (appropriately) critiques the exaggerated individualism of the late modern West, and argues that a more Durkheimian appreciation for social bonds is needed, yet he also admits that this approach, if it became "a normative definition," "would give high marks to fascist and communist societies as well as to cults, so long as

[20] Haidt, *The Righteous Mind*, xxii.

they achieved high levels of cooperation by creating a shared moral order."[21] He is clearly out of his depth in the realm of moral philosophy. As John Gray puts it in his rather scathing review of Haidt, *The Righteous Mind* is an airport tract "promising solutions to problems that have baffled the greatest minds...by sprinkling the magic dust of science on our disorders."[22]

From the perspective of the religious tradition that Haidt gestured toward with his quotation from the Gospel of Matthew, his central error is to not realize that what he is describing is not *human nature*, but, *fallen* human nature. The elephant is not the appropriate metaphor for the human condition as such, but rather for the human soul untethered from God and undisciplined by the habits of virtue. It is possible for human beings to genuinely repent, grow, change, mature, and thus live their lives according to different principles than they did before. It is possible for reason, appropriately understood as the virtues of understanding and prudence, to rightly guide the horse that is the emotions, the intuition, and the will. There are glimpses here and there in the book that Haidt recognizes this and actually longs for it; but they remain only glimpses. To admit that Plato was right after all would be too humiliating.

It is interesting to note that what I have described earlier in this book as dimensional anthropology does actually appear on Haidt's radar screen. He describes "three major clusters of moral themes . . . the ethics of autonomy, community, and divinity." "The ethic of *autonomy* is based on the idea that people are, first and foremost, autonomous individuals with wants, needs, and preferences." "The ethic of *community* is based on the idea that people are, first and foremost, members of larger entities such as families, teams, armies, companies, tribes, and nations." "The ethic of *divinity* is based on the idea that people are, first and foremost, temporary vessels within which a divine soul has been implanted. People are not just animals with an extra serving of consciousness; they are children of God and should behave accordingly."[23] Haidt understands that the late modern West is subtly imperialistic by assuming that its own exaltation of individual autonomy is parochial and narcissistic, but he does not really know what to do with this insight or with the larger framework of dimensional anthropology.

Haidt mentions abortion as one of those topics about which liberals and conservatives have such difficulty engaging in productive conversations,

---

[21] Haidt, *The Righteous Mind*, 316.

[22] John Gray, "The Knowns and the Unknowns," *The New Republic* 243, no. 7 (May 10, 2012) 37.

[23] Haidt, *The Righteous Mind*, 116–17.

but he has nothing substantive to say about it himself. This is an example of the widespread cowardice on this topic in the academic world. To actually have to make an argument, either pro-choice or pro-life or muddled middle, would require making statements that could then be critiqued. It is so much easier just to sit on the sidelines and say "other people should have productive conversations about this."

Haidt's overall message is hobbled by the assumed individualism of much of what passes for "psychology" in today's universities. This problem could have been addressed through reading Girard, who realizes that human beings are deeply mimetic creatures, enmeshed in the lives of others without realizing it. The elephant is not the intuitions of the individual, but the fact that the individual's behavior is being driven by social pressures of which the individual is not conscious. After finishing the book, I did an Internet search for [haidt and girard] which led to an interview in which Haidt was asked if he had read Girard. "No," he said, but "many people have emailed me about him, and I know I need to read him, I think he's vaguely Durkheimian."[24] Such correspondents give me hope.

### *Servais Pinckaers: Freedom for Excellence*

One of the incoherencies of contemporary thought is that a book such as Haidt's will be hailed as a major contribution to human self-understanding, even though its message is primarily deterministic; yet the same people who praise the book will turn around and say that the achievement of completely unfettered individualistic "liberty" is the greatest triumph of the modern liberal political culture. It ought to be clear to us that we need to think about "liberty" more carefully.

*The Sources of Christian Ethics* by the Belgian Dominican scholar Servais Pinckaers is a survey of the history of Western moral thought, written from the point of view of Aquinas' moral realism. His arguments mesh well with and expand upon the insights of Weaver regarding the devastating effects of William of Ockham's nominalism on the modern world. Realism sees the grand scope of the cosmos as a complex harmony, a symphony of elements and voices, unfolding through time. Nominalism separates, divides, creates rivalries, and leads to general chaos. In the words of Pinckaers:

> Freedom of indifference created individualism. It severed the bonds between individuals in the same way in which it had isolated human acts

[24] Interview with Tyler Cowen, "Jonathan Haidt on Morality, Politics, Disgust, and Intellectual Diversity on Campus," accessed March 29, 2019, https://medium.com/conversations-with-tyler/a-conversation-with-jonathan-haidt-35f76604464a .

> from each other. Society was no longer anything more than an artificial creation and a constraint. Henceforth the individual and society would be opposed and would engage in a struggle for power, in a dialectic of domination. The two poles were individual freedom to the point of anarchy and state control to the point of despotism.[25]

At the heart of Pinckaers' book are two key chapters entitled "Freedom of Indifference" and "Freedom for Excellence." "Freedom of Indifference" is the concept at work in nominalism. Because there are no objective moral truths woven into the fabric of the cosmos, freedom means, in the last analysis, doing whatever you want to do. The part about ". . . as long as you don't harm others" becomes weakened to the point of obsolescence, as Nazism, Communism, and abortion have proven. It is the mind that needs to be utterly free in order for freedom of indifference to be the guiding philosophy, and the mind can always define "the others" in such a way that their killing is seen as acceptable in the eyes of those who are doing the killing. Freedom for excellence, in contrast, is a vision that seeks to move human beings out of their native egotism and onto a pathway of spiritual growth. Just as learning to play the piano well takes thousands of hours of disciplined practice, so also does growth in moral maturity take the dedicated effort of years of serious striving to develop the virtues of the human soul. Human beings are not born as competent moral reasoners as their automatic default setting. Growth in virtue is needed before genuine freedom as a human being can be attained. Without that growth human beings are enslaved to various addictions and forms of unrecognized violence.

*Shelby Steele: On Racism*

Shelby Steele is an African-American public intellectual whose book *Shame: How America's Past Sins Have Polarized Our Country* makes an important contribution to understanding our current cultural situation. Steele has suffered the impact of racism in his own life, as he recounts at various points in the book, and he is of course aware of the ongoing effects of racism in areas such as police brutality against persons of color. He is just as critical of these things as any other right-thinking person is. Yet his main object of criticism in the book is the way in which the liberal intelligentsia uses the history of racism in America as a rhetorical tool to further its own power,

---

[25] Servais Pinckaers, *The Sources of Christian Ethics* (Washington, D.C.: Catholic University of America Press, 1995) 351. Patrick Deneen's widely read book *Why Liberalism Failed* (New Haven: Yale University Press, 2018) is an extended meditation on this last point, regarding individual anarchy and state despotism.

while refusing to see reality clearly. There is an unacknowledged hypocrisy at work in liberalism that his book works to expose.

The roots of our current malaise and cultural incoherence, Steele argues, can be traced back to the 1960s. During that era the Vietnam War and the Civil Rights Movement "cracked the veneer of American innocence" and exposed our national hypocrisy.[26] We claimed to be the good guys but could no longer rationalize away our entanglement in evil. This era "bifurcated" moral authority in the United States by opening up a social space in which people could be against militarism, against racism, and for feminism (and the legalization of abortion). This cluster of issues, with others such as environmentalism added on, became a new form of innocence that called itself "progressivism"; anyone who was not on board with its ideology could then be branded as a reactionary, an oppressor, a Neanderthal. This is the pattern that has unfolded up to the present day in the struggle between Democrats and Republicans to win the hearts and minds of the American people. Over time, the original goal of progressivism, which was to call American culture to live up to the ideals that were present in the Declaration of Independence and the Constitution, subtly changed and hardened into the idea that anyone who did not buy into the ideology of progressivism must be guilty of "characterological evil"; they must be incorrigible and thus condemnable, while the progressive finds his or her own psychological affirmation by "dissociating" from the reactionaries:

> A result of this generation's explicit knowledge of America's historical evils was to make social and political morality a more important measure of character than private morality. In the 1950s, your private morality was the measure of your character; in the 1960s, your stance against war, racism, and sexism became far more important measures. . . . Sleep with whomever you wanted, explore your sexuality, expand your mind with whatever drug you liked, forego marriage, follow your instincts and impulses as inner truths, enjoy hedonism as a kind of radical authenticity. The only important thing was that you were dissociated from American evil. Dissociation from this evil became a pillar of identity for my generation.[27]

---

[26] Shelby Steele, *Shame: How America's Past Sins Have Polarized Our Country* (New York: Basic Books, 2015) 56.

[27]Steele, *Shame*, 110–11.

Thus a new form of (unseen) hypocrisy was born. College campuses today are plastered with posters that say "What to do if you are a victim of date rape" not because the reactionaries had their way, but because the liberals did. Our culture is awash in pornography, STDs, sexual harassment in the workplace, and unwanted pregnancies not because traditional notions of moral restraint and virtue won out, but because they were bulldozed by the steamroller of the new progressive orthodoxy. Steele, and the present author, are not going to be holding our breath waiting for a lone progressive to raise his or her hand and say "It's our fault."

Steele says that "dissociation is an artificial virtue because its entire reason for being is to avoid the selflessness, sacrifice, and risk that true virtue inevitably involves. It gives us a road to the decency and legitimacy we want while sparing us the difficulty and struggle of true virtue."[28] Here his message dovetails with that of Pinckaers, who exposits the classical Aristotelian and Thomistic vision of true progress, which is the growth of the soul through its development of the virtues. This is the message that is truly uplifting and enlightening, and it is a message that applies to all human beings regardless of skin color, ethnicity, language, religion, and so forth. The deep irony of today's "liberalism" is that it has put so much energy into dissociation and denunciation of the alleged characterological evil of others that it has blinded itself to its own faults. It has thus done a grave disservice to the African-American community by not being in a position to convey that call to true virtue that everyone needs to hear. Instead, it has expected state-sponsored programs to heal the damage that was inflicted by centuries of racism; the state has no such competence. Paradoxically, liberalism is extreme individualism, but at the same time it is unable to actually lead individuals into the pathway that leads to true health and thriving. Progressivism is stuck on the horizontal plane of identity formation through in-group and out-group rhetorical posturing.

Steele also argues that there is another layer to the philosophical incoherence of today's progressives, namely their embrace of "relativism." This concept is lifted up, primarily with regard to abortion, as the only correct approach thinking about controversial moral issues in a pluralistic society. Those "conservatives" who argue that there are objective moral truths comprehensible through the right exercise of reason are branded as hopeless reactionaries and theocrats. Yet the progressive simply cannot see that relativism was the original sin of the American founding, when the decision was made to allow slavery in the Southern states, because they had a moral phi-

[28]Steele, *Shame*, 140.

losophy that affirmed it. So today, when the pro-choice advocate says that abortion should be legal because "there is no consensus" on this issue, he or she is very precisely echoing the argument made for the legality of slavery.[ There was a pro-slavery book, for example, that included a chapter entitled "Every Man Mind His Own Business."[29] As Steele argues:

> This was the hypocrisy that corrupted our genius for freedom and put us in league with precisely the human impulse to take power through the oppression of others that the American Revolution had challenged. In this sense, "relativizing" was the very essence of American evil. On the one hand, there was the most inspired articulation of human freedom ever rendered, and on the other, the "relativizing" of that freedom so that it was limited by the coarsest of human bigotries—resulting in the denial of freedom to millions.[30]

In Steele's analysis, there are three clear steps that have made possible the rise to cultural power of the "progressive" worldview: 1) relativism, 2) dissociation from the evils of the past, and 3) the "sense of innocence [that] easily translates into moral authority and legitimacy."[31] From within this worldview, Steele can be viewed as nothing other than a "heretic," as he recounts from his own experience of being booed by various audiences of "progressives."[32] Haidt had argued that liberals have a smaller set of moral intuitions than conservatives (harm, justice, and liberty), while conservatives added loyalty, authority, and sanctity. Steele compellingly argues that the narrower set of intuitions is not innocent; they actually result in a hypocritical denunciation of the "characterological evil" of anyone who disagrees with the liberal vision.

### *Daryl Koehn: The Moralistic Way and the Way of Wisdom*

Daryl Koehn's *The Nature of Evil* is a work in the genre of "philosophy and literature." She discusses literary works by Klaus Mann, Patricia Highsmith, R.L. Stevenson, Henry James, and Dante, along with Socrates, Aristotle, and the teachings of Jesus in the New Testament. I focus here on just her introductory remarks, in which she draws a distinction between "the moralistic way and the way of wisdom." Within the moralistic way, which is vastly more common in human beings, evil is identified as the vice, the big-

[29] Calvin Colton, *Abolition, a Sedition: By a Northern Man* (Philadelphia: G.W. Donahue, 1839).

[30] Steele, *Shame*, 148.

[31] Steele, *Shame*, 155.

[32] Steele, *Shame*, 165.

otry, the evil will and intentions of *others*. The persons who follow this way will always see themselves as good and well-intentioned, as innocent. We are good; they are evil. The way of wisdom, which is quite rare in human experience, sees the root of evil as "our lack of self-knowledge." The alleged innocence of the moralistic way is a false identity that leads people to "adopt a variety of self-defeating, violent, paranoid, masochistic, and sadistic strategies. Our lack of self-knowledge locks us into unsatisfying, quasi-mechanical patterns of behavior." She continues that in the moralistic way "we are so busy judging what others have (or have not) done that we do not attend to our behavior. As a result, our reactions and circumstances control us, instead of the reverse. What is more, we often wind up doing—in the name of morality—the very thing for which we condemn others."[33]

It is clear that Koehn's message is attuned to the insights of Girard and Kierkegaard. The moralistic way is the way of the crowd as it continually assumes its own innocence even while it kills scapegoats. Girard is calling his readers to become self-aware, and he shows how great works of literature and the Bible help us to do precisely that. This is Koehn's method also. For Kierkegaard, our greatest need is self-awareness, that authentic awakening of the self that can only happen when one abandons the self-righteousness project of the crowd, admits one's own sinfulness before God, and allows oneself to be drawn forward into the adventure of continuing creation. As Koehn puts it: "Our desire to be publicly respectable removes us from the real world of living human beings. Evil de-centers us. When we live for others, we never develop an internal compass directing our lives. . . . evil is a failure to develop."[34] This insight, that evil arises out of immaturity, will remain outside of Haidt's field of vision as long as he remains trapped by scientism.

## Third Topic: The Abortion Debate

### *Kate Greasley: Whose Rationality? Which Person?*

There is an immense literature on abortion, of course, so the choice of just one book cannot completely avoid the charge of arbitrariness. But the one I have chosen has the merit of being a recently published debate book by Kate Greasley and Christopher Kaczor, under the title *Abortion Rights: For and Against*. Each author is able to make their central case in roughly eighty pages, then reply to the other author, then reply to the reply. It would seem

[33] Daryl Koehn, *The Nature of Evil* (New York : Palgrave Macmillan, 2005) 1–2.

[34] Koehn, *The Nature of Evil*, 45.

to be an example of exactly the sort of careful conversation about a controversial topic that Haidt is hoping for. Since I agree with Kaczor's pro-life position, I will have little to say about his portion of the text.

Greasley considers the pro-life case that personhood begins at conception, but does not find it convincing in any of its iterations. She concedes, however, that if it were convincing, then the argument she presents would collapse: "...if the fetus is a person, equivalent in value to a born human being, then abortion is almost always morally wrong and legal permissions almost entirely unjustified."[35] She does agree that there is a real philosophical question at stake here, which entails that she rejects the radically subjective form that the pro-choice stance sometimes adopts. This radical subjectivism or extreme individual relativism would maintain that if a woman is pregnant and she wants to be pregnant, then there is a person inside of her; if she does not want to be pregnant, then there is not a person inside of her. Personhood is, on this account, completely a product of the will of the woman.[36] Greasley's main argument builds up to the assertion that personhood begins at birth, which she describes as a legal stipulation, a decision made by society. She presents this as "an adequately precise threshold that is clear, practical, and capable of guiding behavior."[37] She thus rules out infanticide but does allow for very late term abortions, in those rare circumstances when they would be desired by the woman or medically indicated. Generally speaking, pro-choice advocates define personhood as consisting in achieved psychological capabilities such as self-awareness, ability to communicate, rationality, and so forth; Greasley admits that this is a high bar that is not met by newborns, but is comfortable landing on the position that a newborn is sufficiently developed in terms of brain activity to be thought of as no longer being in the sub-personal category of "fetus." By virtue of being outside of the woman's body, a newborn is clearly a member of human society, and should therefore be treated as a person bearing the right to life. The overall tone of her argument admits that this whole question of "personhood" is fuzzy because of the tiny changes in the fetus and the newborn day by day; yet, for the purposes of abortion policy and law in modern societies a line has to be drawn somewhere.

---

[35] Kate Greasley and Christopher Kaczor, *Abortion Rights: For and Against* (New York: Cambridge University Press, 2018) 5.

[36]See, for example, Marjorie Reiley Maguire, "Personhood, Covenant, and Abortion," in *Abortion and Catholicism: The American Debate*, ed. Patricia Beattie Jung and Thomas A. Shannon, (New York: Crossroad, 1988) 100–20.

[37] Greasley, *Abortion Rights*, 73–74.

As is the case with many pro-choice authors, Greasley employs bizarre hypothetical scenarios as she makes her argument. One is the "Embryo Rescue Case," in which a person must choose to rescue either five frozen embryos or one born baby from a burning building. Another is the "Intelligent Aliens" thought experiment, that imagines human beings developed the ability to travel to other parts of the galaxy and discovered there intelligent beings capable of rational thinking, communication, emotional engagements, and so forth; these would have to be deemed "persons" even though they were not members of the human species; therefore membership in the human species is clearly not identical with personhood, as pro-life advocates claim. (This is an obviously weak argument, because pro-life advocates do not claim that human beings are the only possible persons in the universe; rather, they claim that if there were other intelligent beings then it would also be wrong for *them* to abort *their* young.) The next hypothetical thought experiment referred to by Greasley is the "Transgenic Spectrum," a notion invented by Jeff McMahan that imagines the genes of chimpanzees being manipulated so that they become closer and closer to human beings, until they become "fully human" in terms of their genetic makeup. This is supposed to be another way of defeating the pro-life position by disconnecting species membership from personhood and emphasizing reasoning ability and self-awareness, which could theoretically be possessed by chimps.[38]

From the pro-life point of view, spending as many pages as Greasley does on such hypothetical scenarios is indicative of the faultiness of pro-choice thinking in general. The most famous pro-choice essay of all, Judith Jarvis Thomson's "A Defense of Abortion," relies on a bizarre scenario in which the reader is supposed to imagine being hooked up via medical tubing to a famous violinist who would die of kidney disease without that arrangement. Pro-life advocates want to talk about the actual lives of human beings, not bizarre hypotheticals. This is illustrated well by the literature of pro-life conversion, which Greasley completely ignores. Norma McCorvey, the "Jane Roe" of the famous abortion case, wrote a book about her conversion to the pro-life side of the fence, which was facilitated by the relationships she developed with pro-life advocates who moved in next to the abortion clinic she was working in at the time. The young daughter of one of the pro-lifers had a great impact on McCorvey, particularly when McCorvey learned that the girl had almost been aborted during a difficult time in the mother's life. [39]

[38] Greasley, *Abortion Rights*, 41–42.

[39] Norma McCorvey, with Gary Thomas, *Won by Love* (Nashville: Thomas Nelson, 1997) 154.

Dr. Bernard Nathanson was an abortionist before *Roe v. Wade*, and one of the key architects of the cultural transformation represented by that decision. In his autobiography, which recounts his conversion to the pro-life cause, he describes in cold, clinical terms how he even aborted a child of which he himself was the father because he did not want his girlfriend to have a baby at that point in their lives. [40] Abby Johnson was the director of an abortion clinic, and she had had two abortions herself before she converted to the pro-life side of the debate. Sue Ellen Browder was a staff writer for *Cosmopolitan* magazine; her autobiography recounts her regretted abortion and her own complicity in the mendacity that was involved in the magazine's promotion of the sexual revolution and abortion rights. [41] Lorraine Murray's autobiography presents the story of her young adult rebellion against her Catholic roots and her chaotic life as a strident feminist and college professor. She also had an abortion that she later came to regret after her conversion to the pro-life cause. [42] Greasley does not display the slightest scintilla of interest in any articles or books of this sort, of which I have only scratched the surface. She has no curiosity about this aspect of the abortion debate, or in the question as to why no pro-life leader has ever had an "epiphany" regarding the truthfulness of the pro-choice worldview and then gone to nursing or medical school with the purpose of then participating in providing abortions. She also has no curiosity about the very extensive literature of pro-life feminism. [43]

Greasley uses rights language, but unreflectively, as is characteristic of the literature on abortion in general, whether it comes from pro-choice or pro-life authors. She asks: "At what point does the immature human being come to possess the right to life?" [44] Her "stipulated" answer to that question is birth. She does not ever ask, however, important questions, such as:

---

[40] Bernard N. Nathanson, *The Hand of God: A Journey from Death to Life by the Abortion Doctor Who Changed His Mind* (Washington, D.C.: Regnery, 1996) 61.

[41] Sue Ellen Browder, *Subverted: How I Helped the Sexual Revolution Hijack the Woman's Movement* (San Francisco: Ignatius Press, 2015).

[42] Lorraine V. Murray, *Confessions of an Ex-Feminist* (San Francisco: Ignatius Press, 2008).

[43] Some examples: Erika Bachiochi, ed., *The Cost of Choice: Women Evaluate the Impact of Abortion* (San Francisco: Encounter, 2004), Mary Krane Derr, Rachel MacNair, and Linda Naranjo-Huebl, eds., *ProLife Feminism: Yesterday and Today*, 2nd ed. (Kansas City, Mo.: Feminism and Nonviolence Studies Association, 2005), Frederica Mathewes-Green, *Real Choices: Listening to Women: Looking for Alternatives to Abortion* (Ben Lomond, Ca.: Conciliar, 1997), Angela Kennedy, ed., *Swimming Against the Tide: Feminist Dissent on the Issue of Abortion* (Dublin: Open Air, 1997).

[44] Greasley, *Abortion Rights*, 170.

"What are rights? Where do they come from? How do we know what rights are and where they come from? What is the history of rights language and how is that history relevant to contemporary debates?" She seems to assume that the concept of a "right" is obvious and agreed upon; the only question is when a human being begins to be a possessor of rights. But in reality, the pro-choice and pro-life worldviews arise out of profoundly different ways of answering this list of questions. The worldviews do not actually agree on what a right is as a philosophical concept. The pro-life author in this book, Christopher Kaczor, does not raise meta-ethical questions about rights language either, unfortunately. If he had, the book would have been much more interesting and beneficial to the reader.

The philosophical errors at work in Greasley's argument are mostly buried and out of sight; they are the assumptions that ground her worldview. For example, the many pages of discussion of bizarre hypotheticals are basically a way of throwing up dust in front of the reader's vision to distract attention from thinking clearly about the science of DNA. The pro-choice way of thinking assumes a constructionist paradigm, within which the process of gestation is implicitly compared to a car factory. The chassis, suspension, tires, engine, interior, and body of the automobile are pieced together in the process of construction. We can then ask the question: "At what point in time has a 'new car' come into existence?" Is it when all the parts are there and it could be started? Or when it actually is started? Or when it rolls out of the factory door for the first time? [45] The pro-choice worldview assumes a metaphysical dualism within which the body is one thing and the mind is another; it is the mind that constitutes "personhood." But there would be no mind without the brain having developed over time. The basic error in the constructionist paradigm is that the human being developing in the womb is not an inert object being constructed by external agents; the inhabitant of the womb is developing him or herself, and the force driving this process is the unique DNA code of the individual. Greasley employs the "heap of sand" argument thinking that it helps her cause. One grain of sand does not constitute a heap, but if more grains are added one by one, then eventually there will be a heap, but "we cannot pinpoint an exact moment when this occurs." [46] This is supposed to establish that the beginning of personhood cannot be pinpointed, but it merely shows that Greasley is unable to grasp

[45] This analogy is developed by Richard Stith, "Construction vs. Development: Polarizing Models of Human Gestation," *Kennedy Institute of Ethics Journal* 24, no. 4 (2014): 345–84.

[46] Greasley, *Abortion Rights*, 72.

the reality that the inhabitant of the womb is not an inert object like a grain of sand. Pro-life advocates love to talk about DNA because they know that the science of the issue is on their side when it is placed within a sound philosophical framework. The inhabitant of the womb is not a potential person but a person with potential. It is the intentional attack on this potential that is the essential moral wrongness of abortion. Pro-choice advocates prefer to live within the pre-scientific worldview in which the inhabitant of the womb is described in dehumanizing terms as a "blob of cells" or "the products of conception."

Rhetoric is key to the abortion debate, of course, and what pro-choice advocates cannot think, without suffering a mental breakdown, is that they are engaged in the same sort of "othering" that is seen in parallel historical situations such as slavery and the Holocaust. Slavery and racism were rooted in a "vertical othering" that drew on the imagery of the Great Chain of Being, and assumed that the "white race" was superior to the "black race." There are many examples of "horizontal othering," in which membership in ethnic groups, tribes, or religions serves as the basis for saying that the group that "we" belong to is superior to the group that "they" belong to. In the wake of World War II, Western culture has turned powerfully in the direction of individualism as the ideology that is supposedly an improvement upon the vertical and horizontal mistakes of the past. But the heart of the pro-choice philosophical stance is "temporal othering" within the trajectory of the life of the individual. Those individuals who are older label themselves as "persons" and grant to themselves "rights," including the right to kill: this act of identity formation is at the same time the expulsion of the younger human beings, the embryos and fetuses, from the realm of personhood and rights. The word "othering" means defining human beings external to oneself as inferior to oneself. This mental act can occur within the vertical axis, the horizontal plane, or the trajectory through time of the individual.

The pro-choice ideology arises out of two unexamined assumptions. The first is that there must be amnesia regarding one's own coming into existence in a womb; the second is that the future trajectory of development of the inhabitant of the womb must not be allowed to carry any substantive weight that would actually limit the complete and utter freedom of choice of the atomized modern self. The killing of the "fetus" must always be justified on the basis of how it is being labeled now, at this moment in time when the killing is happening.

The dehumanizing language employed by pro-choice advocates arises out of the unexamined assumption that the inhabitant of the womb is a piece of property that is owned by the woman who is pregnant, and she can decide to destroy this piece of property that she owns. There is no law built into the fabric of the universe that mandates that human beings must think that way. They can think otherwise; [47] they *ought* to think otherwise. They ought to inhabit an epistemology of love, care, and openness to new life, and reject the false modern ideology of domination of nature and lethal control of other human beings. There is a vast and growing literature criticizing those thought patterns that justify human beings viewing themselves as domineering lords over *nature*. It is deeply ironic that many of the authors of such works support the pro-choice position without realizing that it is one more example of what they are criticizing.

*Stewardship* not *ownership* is the basic attitude toward inhabiting our glorious and mysterious cosmos that corresponds with the health of human spirit. Arguments such as Greasley's are not truly philosophical, in the deep sense of arising out of a love of wisdom; rather, they are symptoms of our present day individual and cultural illness, which Kierkegaard called *the sickness unto death*. For Greasley, *homo sapiens* and *homo necans* [humans as rational knowers and as killers] are concepts that merge, because the chief role of reason is to enable human beings to continually persuade themselves that the violence they do is justified in their own eyes. This is an example of what Haidt meant by the rider on the elephant.

### *Chantal Delsol: Our Inability to Learn the Moral Lessons of History*

Seen from a certain angle, Chantal Delsol's *The Unlearned Lessons of the Twentieth Century* is a kind of philosophical horror story in which it turns out that we, the readers, are the source of the horror, rather than being those who are self-righteously triumphing over it. Delsol's central thesis is that we think that we have overcome and left behind the errors of two great totalitarianisms of the twentieth century, Nazism and Communism, but we have not. "Late modernity has rejected the terrorist aspects of totalitarianism, but it has not abandoned the ideological underpinnings of totalitarianism itself."[48] "The repetition of a crime is avoided only by exposing the subterranean foundation that gave rise to it, by undoing its hidden dynamics," not by blaming our ancestors or "those evil people over there" and distancing ourselves from them.[49] The utopian nightmares of the twentieth century "rested

[47] Along these lines, the thought of René Girard is applied to the topic of abortion in: Bernadette Waterman Ward, "Abortion as a Sacrament: Mimetic Desire and Sacrifice in Sexual Politics." *Contagion* 7 (2000):18–35.

[48] Delsol, *The Unlearned Lessons of the Twentieth Century* (ICS, 2006) 8–9.

[49] Delsol, *Unlearned Lessons*, 22.

on the myth of self-creation, self-foundation, and on the self-sufficiency of mankind."[50] We are continuing this nightmare; the only change is the shape-shifting move from collectivism to individualism and "autonomy." "It is as if the nihilism of late modernity were pursuing the uncompleted work of utopian ideologies."[51] "We may have rejected totalitarian terrorism; we have not restored the common world that is postulates destroyed."[52] We prefer living in that destroyed world. "In the wasteland grows a society of individuals without depth, without their own ideas, without habits of questioning, without distance from themselves, yet who all the while assert their sublime liberty."[53]

The book draws a central contrast, between the current state of our souls, which is immature and narcissistic, and the more mature authentic persons that we could become if we were to actually learn the moral lessons that should have been learned in the twentieth century. In our immaturity, we presume that we are self-sufficient, that we have "the alpha and omega" of truth, automatically, without any striving and growing.[54] This self-satisfied condition can take various forms, such as political or religious fundamentalism, or secular individualism. These are all variations on a theme. "The self-founded individual has nothing to look forward to: he believes he already possesses everything....Self-sufficient man acts solely out of self-preservation." In contrast, the growing person, the authentic moral subject "has an intimate sense that he is incomplete, only half-created."[55] This is a clear echo of Kierkegaard's message in *The Sickness unto Death*; selfhood is a process of growth toward an ideal, and the source of the ideal lies beyond the self itself. We become more fully human and move toward genuine freedom when we respond to the Creator, when we realize that the book of Genesis has deeper insights into our condition than modern intellectuals such as Kant, Rousseau, Mill, or Marx. Modernity thinks that its "freedom" is achieved by abandoning the concept of original sin, but the consequences of that move are paradoxically disastrous. To reject original sin is to 1) believe that evil can be eliminated through a utopian scheme of social engineering, and 2) to "situate the cause of evil somewhere else."[56] The immature self reinforces its belief in its own complete innocence, and will always find a

---

[50] Delsol, *Unlearned Lessons*, 30.
[51] Delsol, *Unlearned Lessons*, 39.
[52] Delsol, *Unlearned Lessons*, 59.
[53] Delsol, *Unlearned Lessons*, 95.
[54] Delsol, *Unlearned Lessons*, 99.
[55] Delsol, *Unlearned Lessons*, 121.
[56] Delsol, *Unlearned Lessons*, 175.

scapegoat to attack outside the self. The narcissistic self will become a god in its own eyes, and always justify whatever form of violence it thinks is necessary to control reality and make it conform to the self's will. That violence may be collectivist or individualist.

This summary has only scratched the surface of this profoundly rich meditation on our situation in the late modern West. If Greasley had read Delsol and framed her defense of abortion as a response to her, then Greasley's text would have been much more interesting.

*Giorgio Agamben: Seizing Power Over Life*

It is common for pro-choice advocates to say that the legalization of abortion is a great step forward in moral progress, because now "women have control over their biology." Giorgio Agamben's book *Homo Sacer: Sovereign Power and Bare Life* shows how what people think is a good argument is actually a horrifically bad one.

In ancient Greek, there were two words that are now translated into English as "life." *Zoe* meant bare physical life; that which is seen in plants, animals, and human beings when they are alive, not dead. *Bios* meant the life of a human being lived within the moral community and protected by the law against homicide. *Zoe* is nature, *bios* is culture. In the ancient world, it tended to be the case that it was the ruling sovereign, the monarch, the governor, or the military general, who had the authority to declare that a particular human being had been demoted from the realm of *bios* to the realm of *zoe*; after that, anyone could kill that individual without being guilty of homicide. The individual had been declared to be "outside the law," an outlaw. As Agamben argues, "the sovereign is the point of indistinction between violence and law, the threshold on which violence passes over into law and law passes over into violence." [57]

Agamben's book traces the workings of this sovereign power from the ancient world up to the Holocaust, in which Hitler demoted the Jews from *bios* to *zoe*. The notion that there can be a "human life unworthy of life" actually preceded Hitler's rise to power. He simply took the notion of euthanasia for the mentally disabled and extended it to genocidal proportions. As with Chantal Delsol, Agamben is skeptical about the notion that Western democracies operate according to a different underlying principle than that

[57] Giorgio Agamben, *Homo Sacer: Sovereign Power and Bare Life* (Stanford: Stanford University Press, 1998) 32.

which animated totalitarianism.[58] It is common in the modern world for people to condemn the barbarities of the past, such as the Crusades, the Inquisition burning heretics at the state, the wars of religion, slavery, and so forth; but what we cannot think, without suffering a meltdown, is the idea that if we have not actually grown in the realm of substantive personal virtue, then we will be reenacting the barbarities of the past unwittingly. Modern democracy does not change the practice of human beings pushing other human beings down from *bios* into *zoe* so that they can be killed with impunity; it simply universalizes the practice; it makes available to everyone. Now we are all monarchs in our own individualistic realms: "In modern biopolitics, sovereign is he [or she] who decides on the value or the nonvalue of life as such."[59]

In the chapter "The Camp as the Nomos of the Modern" Agamben describes how the concentration camps of the Nazis and the Communists display biopolitics in action. He says that

> The correct question to pose concerning the horrors committed in the camps is, therefore, not the hypocritical one of how crimes of such atrocity could be committed against human beings. It would be more honest and, above all, more useful to investigate carefully the juridical procedures and deployments of power by which human beings could be so completely deprived of their rights and prerogatives that no act committed against them could appear any longer as a crime.[60]

When we realize that the abortion clinic is the "camp" of our age where human beings are treated as mere "parasites,"[61] as nothing but biological matter to be killed, then it is hard to imagine a clearer summary of the philosophical underpinnings of the legalization of abortion in the late modern West than the central argument in this book by Agamben. Unwittingly, pro-choice advocate Marjorie Reiley Maguire supports this conclusion, when she says:

---

[58] "Once their fundamental referent becomes bare life [zoe], traditional political distinctions (such as those between Right and Left, liberalism and totalitarianism, private and public) lose their clarity and intelligibility and enter into a zone of indistinction. The ex-communist ruling classes' unexpected fall into the most extreme racism (as in the Serbian program of 'ethnic cleansing') and the rebirth of new forms of fascism in Europe also have their roots here." Agamben, *Homo Sacer*, 122.

[59] Agamben, *Homo Sacer*, 142.

[60] Agamben, *Homo Sacer*, 171.

[61] "...the fetal mode of growth and survival fits the technical definition of *parasite*." Emphasis in original; from a pro-choice article by Joyce Arthur, "No, Virginia, Abortion Is NOT Genocide," *The Humanist*, July/August 2000, 21.

> [E]ven if the fetus is a person and thus does have a moral right to bodily integrity, the fetus is beyond the protection of the law. The fetus can be compared to a citizen of a totalitarian state whose freedom is taken away by the government. As a free society we would like the inhabitants of foreign countries to experience freedom. However, because we do not want to destroy our own society by imposing democracy on another government, we tolerate systems of government which are different than our own, and even governments we abhor. Similarly, a woman's body is like the borders of a foreign country. [62]

In this quotation, the political theory underlying the pro-choice position is laid out as clearly and candidly as it possibly could be.

Agamben does not mention abortion explicitly in this book under consideration, or anywhere else in his writings. However, pro-life advocates will be intrigued by this comment: "Until a new and coherent ontology of potentiality has replaced the ontology founded on the primacy of actuality and its relation to potentiality, a political theory freed from the aporias of sovereignty remains unthinkable."[63] Pro-choice advocates love to wield the word "potentiality" as a sword that kills off the dignity and worth of the inhabitant of the womb. The thought that they cannot allow themselves to think is that they are viewing the world through upside-down spectacles. Our current "actuality" is that we are radical individualists who always justify our violence in our own eyes. This "actuality" does not deserve the sovereign power that it gives to itself. We are the guilty crowd killing the innocent scapegoat, the one who cannot defend him or herself.

### *Søren Kierkegaard: Mutiny Against the Creator*

David Bentley Hart's fine essay "Christ and Nothing (No Other God)" makes the point that in the modern world many people think that they are "secular," but they are mistaken.[64] The cumulative influence of Judaism and Christianity over the past 3,000 years has acted as an acid dissolving all of the old gods; the only god left is the self, itself. That is the late modern West, in a nutshell.

Kierkegaard's thought, as I have shown in this book, focuses intently on human rebellion against the ongoing divine work of creation. We do not

---

[62] Marjorie Reiley Maguire, "Symbiosis, Biology, and Personalization," in *Abortion Rights and Fetal "Personhood"* ed. Edd Doerr and James W. Prescott, (Long Beach, Ca.: Centerline, 1989) 12–13.

[63] Agamben, Homo Sacer, 44.

[64] Published in Hart, *In the Aftermath: Provocations and Laments* (Grand Rapids: Eerdmans, 2009).

want to allow God to create us; we do not want to become our true selves before God. We thus exist in a state of mutiny against God.[65] This is our *subjective* state, but it leads also to *objective* consequences. Our rebellion against God is the deepest root of our violence against other human beings. We wish that we could slay God to silence the voice of creation, but we cannot. God is out of our reach. The best we can do, which is also the worst we can do, is to kill other human beings made in the image of God and loved by God.

As if it is necessary to point out the obvious, in our age these deep motives of the misshapen human heart are clearly seen in abortion. The creation of a new human being is the work of God. We human beings express our rebellion against God by attacking this work. To say that we are usurping the role of God by taking lethal power into our own hands is correct, but it needs to be clarified a bit further. It is not simply that we are "playing God" through abortion; rather, we are playing the role of a *violent* God that has been generated by our own idolatrous imagination. The true God is *nonviolent*, loving, giving, forgiving, compassionate, creative, beautiful, and good. The true God has been revealed to us in Jesus Christ.

### *The Kierkegaard-Girard Option*

So what is the Kierkegaard-Girard Option? These bullet points begin to outline the answer:

- We *must* think about the question "Why are human beings violent?" The luxury of ignorance is no longer possible. This question needs to be asked as a society-wide inquiry, built into our curricula at the high school and college levels, and also in seminaries. This is the crucial element in the New Copernican Revolution.
- The abortion debate will take a turn in a strongly pro-life direction at some point in the future, because the pro-choice worldview arises out of the philosophical falsity of othering. We need to prepare as a culture for this major change.
- The debate over same-sex marriage will likely be a "We will have to agree to disagree" situation for a long time into the future. Thinking about the difference between parallel vs. conflictual competition will be helpful. Which worldview leads to healthier communities that contribute to the flourishing of human lives?

---

[65] Kierkegaard, *Works of Love*, 117.

- The notion that "liberals" can win the culture wars and then become oppressors of "conservatives" is not a viable pathway into the future.
- Those on the cultural left and right need to find ways to have more productive conversations going into the future; these conversations need to be informed by the insights of the most subtle and brilliant anthropological thinkers of the modern world, such as Kierkegaard and Girard (and the other authors referred to in this chapter, along with many others I did not have time to mention).

*Commentary*

1. In our formal educational system, from kindergarten up through high school, we have spirited debates over the merits of standardized testing in subjects such as math, language arts, social studies, and science. It does not seem to occur to us, however, that there ought to be another element of the curriculum: thinking about why human beings are violent. I am not referring to anti-bullying programs, which are of course necessary and beneficial. To treat other human beings unethically is obviously a travesty, and schools ought to shape their students in a positive way at that very basic level of human decency. I am talking about the need for anthropological self-understanding. There can and ought to be age-appropriate instruction all along the way that will get the students thinking about the phenomenon of violence in human behavior. At the college level there should be a required course on this topic, with more advanced readings and concepts. Seminaries should train the religious leaders of the future in how to lead their congregations to think about this topic. If this fundamental change in our curriculum were to be implemented, then we could begin to talk about a New Copernican Revolution. Copernicus is a symbol for the development of the modern natural sciences; that is an understanding of the world external to ourselves. What we urgently need is internal self-understanding as human beings. We need to wrestle profoundly with this question: Why are we violent? If we take up what I am calling the Kierkegaard-Girard Option, then we will be at the forefront of this wrestling.

2. There is no way that I can soften the blow of what I will say next. The pro-choice way of thinking is philosophically corrupt, just as the defense of slavery was. It is another form of dehumanizing othering that is working against the grain of genuine moral progress in history. Forms of philosophical falsity, when they are adopted unwittingly by large numbers of people, have shown themselves to be capable of living on for centuries. But eventually they crumble and collapse. That will happen at some point in the

future with the pro-choice way of thinking. We need to prepare for that eventuality. This will involve changing our current ways of thinking no matter who we are and how we think about abortion presently. It will be a vast upheaval, an "apocalypse" for individualism. It will require rethinking many different aspects of education, employment, sexuality, religion, government, and medicine. When the spell that currently holds us is broken, we will wake up in a new world. We need to learn from the past that the ending of slavery did not end racism; it was followed by Jim Crow and the lynching tree. We need to do things differently this time around. We need to not see ourselves as "winners" or "losers" of an argument, but as human beings who need to change in major ways so that our society becomes a culture that protects all human lives and rejects all forms of philosophical dehumanization. I am not optimistic that we are up to the task, but optimism is not what we need; *hope* is what we need.

3. Same-sex marriage, or "marriage equality," as its proponents prefer to describe it, is an issue that lays bare the problem of epistemology. How do you know what you claim to know is the truth?

On the traditionalist side, there is often a resort to what are called by the other side the "clobber verses" in the Bible, that say homosexual activity is sinful. The progressive side is familiar with all of these verses and is not impressed with or persuaded by them. Those intellectuals on the traditionalist side who realize that more is needed than mere proof-texting usually think and argue within what could be called a kind of Christian Taoism. I am consciously alluding here to C.S. Lewis' work *The Abolition of Man*, which used "The Tao" as a stand-in for the traditional Christian idea of the natural law. There is a moral order built into the universe, that human reason is able to comprehend, and within this order there is a complementarity of male and female.[66] Verses such as Genesis 1:27 "So God created man in his own image, in the image of God created he him; male and female created he them (KJV)," and Jesus' comments on divorce in Mark 10 are quoted not so much as proof-texts but rather as anthropological worldview texts.

> "It was because your hearts were hard that Moses wrote you this law," Jesus replied. "But at the beginning of creation God 'made them male and female.' 'For this reason a man "will leave his father and mother and be united to his wife, and the two will become one flesh.' So they are no

---

[66] See, for example, Helen Alvaré and Stephen Lopes, eds., *Not Just Good, but Beautiful: The Complementary Relationship Between Man and Woman* (Walden, N.Y.: Plough, 2015), which has chapters by Protestant and Catholic authors (including Pope Francis), a Jew, a Muslim, a Buddhist, a Hindu, a Taoist, and a Mormon.

> longer two, but one flesh. Therefore what God has joined together, let no one separate." (Mark 10:5–9 NIV)

For the traditionalist, the modern world's central principle is the rejection of natural law; it makes sense that the authority of the Bible would be rejected by progressives, and also the authority of reason, which is understood as mental attunement with the moral order of the cosmos. Moderns seek radical individual autonomy and they tear asunder the traditional understanding of marriage as a joining together of man and woman in a lifelong bond of love that is open to procreation. The modernists, from this point of view, redefine "marriage" as a contract between consenting adults, regardless of gender or "gender identity."

The progressives respond to this argument with—wait for it—a *natural law* argument of their own. They argue that God has created some people with an in-built same-sex orientation. This sounds strange to traditionalist ears, but for progressives, this is the correct way to think anthropologically. This is testified to through the experience of those who have this orientation. The cornerstone of epistemology has become human experience, rather than scripture or "reason" as it has been construed in previous centuries. There is now a modern "reason" that sees things differently. And when the argument is made in theological terms, the further claim is made that the acceptance of same-sex relationships and marriage is the new work that God is doing in our age; this is the Holy Spirit speaking to us, informing us that the traditional model of heteronormativity is outdated, oppressive, and harmful to the flourishing of human beings who are all of sacred worth in the eyes of God. God does not always create heterosexual human beings; rather, there is great variety in God's creative work, with regard to the shaping of human hearts and their attractions.

There is already a large and growing literature in this debate. On the traditionalist side, there are books such as:

Sherif Girgis, Ryan Anderson, and Robert George, *What Is Marriage?: Man and Woman: A Defense*, (Encounter, 2012).

Robert R. Reilly, *Making Gay Okay: How Rationalizing Homosexual Behavior Is Changing Everything*, (Ignatius, 2014).

Eve Tushnet, *Gay and Catholic: Accepting My Sexuality, Finding Community, Living My Faith*, (Ave Maria Press, 2014).

Daniel Mattson, *Why I Don't Call Myself Gay: How I Reclaimed My Sexual Reality and Found Peace*, (Ignatius, 2017).

Todd Wilson, *Mere Sexuality: Rediscovering the Christian Vision of Sexuality*, (Zondervan, 2017).

The book by Tushnet accepts the idea that some people have an in-built same-sex attraction, but argues that they should live celibate lives.
On the progressive side there are books such as:

James Alison, *Faith Beyond Resentment: Fragments Catholic and Gay*, (Crossroad, 2001).
Patrick Cheng, *Rainbow Theology: Bridging Race, Sexuality, and Spirit*, (New York: Seabury Books, 2013).
Margaret Farley, *Just Love: A Framework for Christian Sexual Ethics*, (Continuum, 2006).
Colby Martin, *UnClobber: Rethinking Our Misuse of the Bible on Homosexuality* (Westminster John Knox, 2016).
David Gushee, *Changing Our Mind*, 3rd ed. (Read the Spirit Books, 2017).

Gushee was for many years a prominent evangelical ethicist, who has departed from that tradition's rejection of the validity of same-sex relationships. I have artificially limited this list to five from each camp; the bibliography could easily be expanded beyond one hundred titles.

Speaking autobiographically, my theological leanings are on the traditionalist side, but I have spent most of my adult life in academic settings that are on the progressive side, and I have personal friendships inside and outside of academia on both sides of the debate. My plea is for a change in rhetoric. Those on the traditionalist side should stop calling those who disagree with them "perverts" and "sodomites," etc.; and those on the progressive side should stop calling those who disagree with them "bigots" motivated by "hatred." Such language is counterproductive.

In the world of sports there are two main types of competition: conflictual and parallel. Conflictual competition is seen in sports like hockey, soccer, basketball, American football, and so forth. There is an object, a puck or a ball, and one team is trying to move it toward one goal, while the other team is trying to move it toward the opposite goal. This conflict can take the form of physical violence that leads to serious injuries, particularly in football. Parallel competition is seen in sports such as sprinting, swimming, and golf. The athletes are trying to do the same thing as their competitors, but faster, or using fewer strokes. I suggest this as a better way of looking at the struggle over sexual ethics within Christianity. There ought to be parallel competition rather than conflictual competition. Which worldview, the traditionalist or the progressivist, can more successfully over the long term form and sustain communities that foster the flourishing of the human beings who make up those communities? The question I am posing is not narrowly focused on issues of sexual ethics, though those are important. Which worldview does better at not only promoting a sound sexual way of being, but also which does better at feeding the hungry, giving water to the thirsty, showing hospitality to strangers, clothing the naked, caring for the sick, and visiting those in prison? See Matthew 25.

The philosophical and theological arguments about same-sex marriage have eloquent and well-educated advocates on all sides. Let us treat one another with civility and charity as we go forward, living out our deep differences in epistemology, while yet treating one another with decency and kindness.

4. The notion that "liberals" can win the culture wars and then become oppressors of "conservatives" is not a viable pathway into the future. That is an example of conflictual rather than parallel competition. James Alison, whose book *Faith Beyond Resentment* was just mentioned a bit earlier, is helpful in this regard. He is a gay man who is a Catholic priest. That puts him in what is by definition an awkward position in relation to the official teaching of the Church, given that he does not accept the idea that all those who have same-sex attractions ought to remain celibate. He affirms the validity of committed same-sex relationships that involve sexual intimacy. Yet he is critical of his fellow progressives when he sees them thinking and acting in ways that seem to arise out of *resentment*, which is a psychological way of being that he wrestles with very deeply in the book. To act out of resentment is to assume a "winners and losers," "good guys and bad guys," "zero-sum" mentality. The traditionalist position on sexual ethics has had the upper hand in Western culture until quite recently. With the dramatic cultural changes that have happened recently in a progressive direction, there is a temptation for progressives to be vindictive, to "give them a taste of their own medicine," to pass and enforce laws that will tighten down the thumb screws on any wedding cake bakers, or photographers, or florists who decline to provide their services to same-sex weddings. There are laws that have been passed that force Catholic social service agencies completely out of the realm of adoption and foster care services if they will not place children with same-sex couples. The issues of constitutional interpretation and church-state relations are complicated and difficult to sort out in this new world. Traditionalists can now play the victim card, and will not be impressed by the rhetoric of "justice" as it is employed by the progressives. They will point out that the moral relativism that is usually argued for by progressives seems to disappear like a puff of smoke in certain circumstances, to be replaced by a hubristic confidence in the moral superiority of the progressives, which justifies their newly passed laws. Patrick Deneen's book *Why Liberalism Failed*

provides interesting perspectives on how the progressivist position is often lived out as individual autonomy and coercive state power advancing hand-in-hand.[67]

I mentioned James Alison's attempt to shoot a warning shot across the bow of this temptation to act out of resentment; Shelby Steele's personal story includes an intriguing parallel, from the traditionalist side. Steele recounts how when he was on his high school's swim team he was intentionally not invited to a particular social gathering of the team solely because he was black. There was an inevitable painful conversation with his coach, in which the coach's role in orchestrating the racism was exposed; his teammates also tried to plead their innocence in the situation, knowing full well that they were not innocent. Steele recounts:

> All moral authority had shifted to me, so that I—unexpectedly—had the power to pronounce on their fundamental human decency. Having colluded in the evil of excluding me (a small betrayal as it related to me, but a profound betrayal as it related to the American creed of fairness, honor, and equality), they had inadvertently bestowed on me the priestly power of dispensation.[68]

Steele had made the decision to quit the team, even though he was the star swimmer. It was not because of the racist incident, but simply because he had grown out of a passionate desire to swim and wanted to move on to other things. But the coach and his teammates were fully convinced that his decision was based on the racist incident. They could not let go of that; but he already had. He did not respond out of resentment and anger. He walked out of the situation, able to let it go and move on. He was not trapped; they were. Progressives and traditionalists ought to listen to Steele and Alison at this intriguing point of intersection between their books.

5. Those on the cultural left and right need to find ways to have more productive conversations going into the future; these conversations need to be informed by the insights of most subtle and brilliant anthropological thinkers of the modern world, such as those I have been drawing on in this chapter.

What is needed is not retreat into cultural (or virtual) enclaves of the like-minded, but an increased ability to have respectful conversations with those who view the world through different lenses, who operate out of different epistemologies and assumptions. Everyone should bring their best arguments and relate the stories of what gives them hope and enkindles their

---

[67] Deneen, *Why Liberalism Failed*, 38.

[68] Steele, *Shame*, 51–52.

love and faith. And everyone should listen with open ears and minds to what is being said by others. We will inevitably have disagreements and we will find solace and support in a community of the like-minded. But the future of the human race as a whole depends on all of us developing the capacity to live our lives out of a generous spirit that draws its energy not from resentment, anger, and self-absorption, but from an openness to the mysterious creative energy of God.

# BIBLIOGRAPHY


Agamben, Giorgio. *Homo Sacer: Sovereign Power and Bare Life*. Translated by Daniel Heller-Roazen. Stanford: Stanford University Press, 1998.

Alvaré, Helen, and Stephen Lopes, eds. *Not Just Good, but Beautiful: The Complementary Relationship Between Man and Woman*. Walden, N.Y.: Plough, 2015.

Appel, Edward C. "Kenneth Burke: Coy Theologian." *Journal of Communication & Religion* 16, no. 2 (1993): 99-110.

Arthur, Joyce. "No, Virginia, Abortion Is NOT Genocide," *The Humanist* (July/August, 2000): 20–23.

Asgill, John. *The Metamorphosis of Man, by the Death and Resurrection of Christ from the Dead*, Part I. London, 1727. Based on information from English Short Title Catalogue. Eighteenth Century Collections Online. Gale Group.

Bachiochi, Erika, ed. *The Cost of Choice: Women Evaluate the Impact of Abortion*. San Francisco: Encounter, 2004.

Barth, Karl. *The Christian Life*. Grand Rapids: Eerdmans, 1981.

Becker, Ernest. *The Denial of Death*. New York: Free Press, 1973.

_____. *Escape from Evil*. New York: Free Press, 1975.

Bellinger, Charles K. "'The Crowd Is Untruth': A Comparison of Kierkegaard and Girard." *Contagion: A Journal of Violence, Mimesis, and Culture* 3 (1996): 103–19.

_____. *The Genealogy of Violence: Reflections on Creation, Freedom, and Evil*. New York: Oxford University Press, 2001.

____. "The Joker Is Satan, and So Are We: Girard and The Dark Knight." *Journal of Religion & Film* 13, Iss. 1, Article 5. Accessed March 30, 2019. https://digitalcommons.unomaha.edu/jrf/vol13/iss1/5 .

_____. *The Trinitarian Self: The Key to the Puzzle of Violence*. Eugene: Pickwick, 2008.

Bolingbroke, Henry St. John. *Remarks on the History of England: By the Right Honourable Henry St. John, Lord Viscount Bolingbroke*. London, 1780. Based on information from English Short Title Catalogue. Eighteenth Century Collections Online. Gale Group.

Booth, Wayne. "Kenneth Burke's Religious Rhetoric: 'God-Terms' and the Ontological Proof." In *Rhetorical Invention and Religious Inquiry: New Perspectives*, edited by Walter Jost and Wendy Olmsted, 25–46. New Haven & London: Yale University Press, 2000.

Browder, Sue Ellen. *Subverted: How I Helped the Sexual Revolution Hijack the Woman's Movement*. San Francisco: Ignatius Press, 2015.

Bubbio, Paolo Diego. *Intellectual Sacrifice and Other Mimetic Paradoxes*. East Lansing: Michigan State University Press, 2018.

Burke, Kenneth. *Attitudes Toward History*, 3rd ed. Berkeley: University of California Press, 1984.

_____. "Definition of Man." *The Hudson Review* 16 (Winter 1963-64): 491–514. [Also in *Language as Symbolic Action*].

_____. *A Grammar of Motives and A Rhetoric of Motives*. Cleveland: World Publishing, 1962.

_____. *Language as Symbolic Action: Essays on Life, Literature, and Method*. Berkeley: University of California Press, 1966.

_____. *Permanence and Change: An Anatomy of Purpose*, 2nd ed. Indianapolis: Bobbs-Merrill, 1965 [originally published in 1935].

_____. *The Philosophy of Literary Form: Studies in Symbolic Action*. Baton Rouge: Louisiana State University Press, 1941.

_____. *The Rhetoric of Religion: Studies in Logology*. Berkeley: University of California Press, 1970.

Burtchaell, James Tunstead. *Rachel Weeping and Other Essays on Abortion*. Kansas City, Kansas: Andrews and McMeel, 1982.

Carter, C. Allen. *Kenneth Burke and the Scapegoat Process*. Norman: University of Oklahoma Press, 1996.

_____. "Logology and Religion: Kenneth Burke on the Metalinguistic Dimension of Language." *Journal of Religion* 72 (January 1992): 1–18.

Cavanaugh, William T. *The Myth of Religious Violence: Secular Ideology and the Roots of Modern Conflict*. New York: Oxford University Press, 2009.

Chesterton, G. K. *Orthodoxy*. Garden City: Doubleday, 1959.

Colton, Calvin. *Abolition, a Sedition: By a Northern Man*. Philadelphia: G.W. Donahue, 1839.

Cowley, Hannah. *A School for Greybeards; Or, the Mourning Bride: A Comedy, in Five Acts*. Dublin, 1787. Based on information from English Short Title Catalogue. Eighteenth Century Collections Online. Gale Group.

Crusius, Timothy W. *Kenneth Burke and the Conversation After Philosophy*. Carbondale: Southern Illinois University Press, 1999.

_____. "The Question of Kenneth Burke's Ethics." *KB Journal* 3/1 (Fall 2006). Accessed March 29, 2019. http://www.kbjournal.org/crusius .

Davies, Thomas. *Memoirs of the Life of David Garrick, Esq. Interspersed with Characters and Anecdotes of His Theatrical Contemporaries*. Dublin, 1780. Based on information from English Short Title Catalogue. Eighteenth Century Collections Online. Gale Group.

Deneen, Patrick. *Why Liberalism Failed*. New Haven: Yale University Press, 2018.

Derr, Mary Krane, Rachel MacNair, and Linda Naranjo-Huebl, eds. *ProLife Feminism: Yesterday and Today*, 2nd ed. Kansas City, Mo.: Feminism and Nonviolence Studies Association, 2005.

Dreher, Rod, *The Benedict Option: A Strategy for Christians in a Post-Christian World*. New York: Sentinel, 2017.

Edwards, Jonathan. *The Nature of True Virtue*. Eugene, Oregon: Wipf & Stock, 2003.

Eller, Vernard. *Kierkegaard and Radical Discipleship: A New Perspective*. Princeton: Princeton University Press, 1968.

Elshtain, Jean Bethke. *Sovereignty: God, State, and Self.* New York: Basic Books, 2008.

Girard, René. *Battling to the End.* East Lansing: Michigan State University Press, 2010.

_____. *Deceit, Desire, and the Novel; Self and Other in Literary Structure.* Translated by Yvonne Freccero. Baltimore: Johns Hopkins University Press, 1965.

_____. "The First Stone," *Renascence* 52 (1999): 5–17.

_____. *The Girard Reader.* Edited by James G. Williams. New York: Crossroad, 1996.

_____. *I See Satan Fall Like Lightning.* Translated by James G. Williams. Maryknoll, N.Y.: Orbis, 2001.

_____. *Mimesis and Theory: Essays on Literature and Criticism, 1953–2005.* Edited by Robert Doran. Stanford: Stanford University Press, 2008.

_____. *The Scapegoat.* Translated by Yvonne Freccero. Baltimore: Johns Hopkins University Press, 1986.

_____. *"To Double Business Bound": Essays on Literature, Mimesis, and Anthropology.* Baltimore: Johns Hopkins University Press, 1978.

_____. *Violence and the Sacred.* Translated by Patrick Gregory. Baltimore: Johns Hopkins University Press, 1977.

Girard, René, Jean–Michel Oughourlian, and Guy Lefort. *Things Hidden since the Foundation of the World.* Translated by Stephen Bann and Michael Metteer. Stanford: Stanford University Press, 1987.

Girard, René, Pierpaolo Antonello, and João Cezar de Castro Rocha. *Evolution and Conversion.* New York: T.&T. Clark, 2007.

Gould, Stephen Jay. *Rocks of Ages: Science and Religion in the Fullness of Life.* New York: Ballantine Books, 2002.

Gourevitch, Philip. *We Wish to Inform You That Tomorrow We Will Be Killed with Our Families: Stories from Rwanda.* New York: Farrar Straus and Giroux, 1998.

Gray, John. "The Knowns and the Unknowns," *The New Republic* 243, no. 7 (May 10, 2012), 33–37.

Greasley, Kate, and Christopher Kaczor. *Abortion Rights: For and Against.* New York: Cambridge University Press, 2017.

Gregory, Brad S. *The Unintended Reformation: How a Religious Revolution Secularized Society.* Cambridge, Mass.: Harvard University Press, 2012.

Haidt, Jonathan. *The Righteous Mind: Why Good People Are Divided by Politics and Religion.* New York: Vintage Books, 2012.

Haidt, Jonathan, and Tyler Cowen. "Jonathan Haidt on Morality, Politics, Disgust, and Intellectual Diversity on Campus." Accessed March 29, 2019. https://medium.com/conversations-with-tyler/a-conversation-with-jonathan-haidt-35f766044640a .

Hamerton-Kelly, Robert. *The Gospel and the Sacred.* Minneapolis: Fortress Press, 1994.

Hamid, Tawfik. *Inside Jihad.* Mountain Lake Park, Md.: Mountain Lake Press, 2015.

Hart, David. *Atheist Delusions: The Christian Revolution and Its Fashionable Enemies.* New Haven: Yale University Press, 2009.

_____. *In the Aftermath: Provocations and Laments.* Grand Rapids: Eerdmans, 2009.

Hughes, Glenn, ed. *The Politics of the Soul: Eric Voegelin on Religious Experience.* Lanham, Md.: Rowman & Littlefield Publishers, 1999.

Husin, Asna. "Islamic Peace Education: Changing Hearts and Minds." In *Crescent and Dove: Peace and Conflict Resolution in Islam.* Edited by Qamar-Ul Huda, 151–78. Washington, D.C.: United States Institute of Peace Press, 2010.

Juergensmeyer, Mark. *Terror in the Mind of God: The Global Rise of Religious Violence*, 4th ed. Berkeley: University of California Press, 2017.

Kaplan, Grant. *René Girard, Unlikely Apologist: Mimetic Theory and Fundamental Theology.* University of Notre Dame Press, 2016.

Kelsey, David H. *Eccentric Existence: A Theological Anthropology.* Louisville: Westminster John Knox Press, 2009.

Kennedy, Angela, ed. *Swimming Against the Tide: Feminist Dissent on the Issue of Abortion.* Dublin: Open Air, 1997.

Kierkegaard, Søren. *Christian Discourses.* Translated by Howard V. Hong and Edna H. Hong. Princeton: Princeton University Press, 1997.

_____. *For Self-Examination ; Judge for Yourself!* Translated by Howard V. Hong, and Edna H. Hong . Princeton: Princeton University Press, 1990.

_____. *The Moment and Late Writings.* Translated by Howard V. Hong, and Edna H. Hong. Princeton: Princeton University Press, 1998.

_____. *The Point of View.* Translated by Howard V. Hong and Edna H. Hong. Princeton: Princeton University Press, 1998.

_____. *Practice in Christianity.* Translated by Howard V. Hong and Edna H. Hong. Princeton: Princeton University Press, 1991.

_____. *The Sickness Unto Death: A Christian Psychological Exposition for Upbuilding and Awakening.* Translated by Howard V. Hong and Edna H. Hong. Princeton: Princeton University Press, 1983.

_____. *Søren Kierkegaard's Journals and Papers.* Edited and translated by Howard V. Hong and Edna H. Hong, assisted by Gregor Malantschuk. Bloomington, Indiana University Press, 1967–78.

_____. *Two Ages: The Age of Revolution and the Present Age : A Literary Review.* Translated by Howard V. Hong and Edna H. Hong. Princeton, N.J: Princeton University Press, 1978.

_____. *Upbuilding Discourses in Various Spirits.* Translated by Howard V. Hong and Edna H. Hong. Princeton: Princeton University Press, 1993.

_____. *Without Authority.* Translated by Howard V. Hong and Edna H. Hong. Princeton: Princeton University Press, 1997.

_____. *Works of Love.* Translated by Howard V. Hong and Edna H. Hong. Princeton: Princeton University Press, 1995.

Koehn, Daryl. *The Nature of Evil.* New York : Palgrave Macmillan, 2005.

Lindsay, Stan A. *Implicit Rhetoric: Kenneth Burke's Extension of Aristotle's Concept of Entelechy.* New York: University Press of America, 1998.

Lynch, Paul. "Something Completely Different: Notes Toward a Burkean Ethics." *KB Journal* 5/1 (Fall 2008). http://www.kbjournal.org/paul_lynch accessed March 29, 2019.

McCorvey, Norma, with Gary Thomas. *Won by Love.* Nashville: Thomas Nelson, 1997.

MacIntyre, Alasdair. *After Virtue: A Study in Moral Theory.* 2nd ed. Notre Dame, Ind.: University of Notre Dame Press, 1984.

McKinnon, Alastair. "Kierkegaard and the 'Leap of Faith,'" *Kierkegaardiana* 16 (1993): 107–25.

Maguire, Marjorie Reiley. "Personhood, Covenant, and Abortion." In *Abortion and Catholicism: The American Debate.* Edited by Patricia Beattie Jung and Thomas A. Shannon, 100–20. New York: Crossroad, 1988.

_____. "Symbiosis, Biology, and Personalization." In *Abortion Rights and Fetal "Personhood."* Edited by Edd Doerr and James W. Prescott, 11–19. Long Beach, Ca.: Centerline, 1989.

Marsden, George. "Challenging the Presumptions of the Age." In *The Legacy of Jonathan Edwards: American Religion and the Evangelical Tradition.* Edited by D.G. Hart, Sean Michael Lucas, and Stephen J. Nichols, 99–113. Grand Rapids: Baker Academic, 2003.

Mathewes-Green, Frederica. *Real Choices: Listening to Women: Looking for Alternatives to Abortion.* Ben Lomond, Ca.: Conciliar, 1997.

Murray, Lorraine V. *Confessions of an Ex-Feminist.* San Francisco: Ignatius Press, 2008.

Nathanson, Bernard N. *The Hand of God: A Journey from Death to Life by the Abortion Doctor Who Changed His Mind.* Washington, D.C.: Regnery, 1996.

Niebuhr, H. Richard. *Theology, History, and Culture: Major Unpublished Writings.* New Haven: Yale University Press, 1996.

Nietzsche, Friedrich W. *On the Genealogy of Morality.* Translated by Carol Diethe. New York: Cambridge University Press, 1994.

Philostratus, Flavius. *The Life of Apollonius of Tyana, The Epistles of Apollonius and the Treatise by Eusebius with an English Translation by F.C. Conybeare*, Loeb Classical Library, Vol. 1. Cambridge, Mass.: Harvard University Press, 1948.

Pinckaers, Servais. *The Sources of Christian Ethics.* Translated by Mary Thomas Noble. Washington, D.C.: Catholic University of America Press, 1995.

Rosenbaum, Ron. *Explaining Hitler: The Search for the Origins of His Evil.* New York: Random House, 1998.

Rossatti, Gabriel Guedes. "Kierkegaard, Hannah Arendt and the Advent of the 'Hollow Men' or Towards a Kierkegaardian Reading of *Eichmann in Jerusalem.*" In *Kierkegaard Studies Yearbook 2014*, edited by Heiko Schulz, 301–28. Berlin: De Gruyter, 2014.

Rueckert, William H. *Kenneth Burke and the Drama of Human Relations*, 2nd ed. Berkeley: University of California Press, 1982.

Steele, Shelby. *Shame: How America's Past Sins Have Polarized Our Country.* New York: Basic Books, 2015.

Stein, Ruth. *For Love of the Father: A Psychoanalytic Study of Religious Terrorism.* Stanford: Stanford University Press, 2010.

Stith, Richard. "Construction vs. Development: Polarizing Models of Human Gestation." *Kennedy Institute of Ethics Journal* 24, no. 4 (2014): 345–84.

Swartley, Willard M., ed. *Violence Renounced: René Girard, Biblical Studies, and Peacemaking.* Telford, Pa.: Pandora Press, 2000.

Thames, Richard H. "The Gordian Not: Untangling the Motivorum." *KB Journal* 3, no. 2 (Spring 2007). Accessed March 29, 2019. http://www.kbjournal.org/thames1.

Vickery, John B., and J'nan M. Sellery, eds. *The Scapegoat: Ritual and Literature.* Boston: Houghton Mifflin, 1972.

Voegelin, Eric. "Configurations of History." In *The Concept of Order*. Edited by Paul Grimley Kuntz, 23–42. Seattle: University of Washington Press, 1968.

_____. *Modernity Without Restraint: The Political Religions, The New Science of Politics, and Science, Politics, and Gnosticism.* Edited by Manfred Henningsen. Columbia: University of Missouri Press, 2000.

_____. *Order and History, Volume 1: Israel and Revelation.* Baton Rouge: Louisiana State University Press, 1956.

Ward, Bernadette Waterman. "Abortion as a Sacrament: Mimetic Desire and Sacrifice in Sexual Politics." *Contagion* 7 (2000): 18–35.

Ward, Bruce Kinsey. *Redeeming the Enlightenment: Christianity and the Liberal Virtues.* Grand Rapids: Eerdmans, 2010.

Weaver, Richard M. *Ideas Have Consequences.* Chicago: University of Chicago Press, 1948.

# Index